THE BUSINESS PLAN WORKBOOK

The Business Plan Workbook
for an Owner-Managed Business

*A practical guide to creating
an effective business plan for an
owner-managed business*

I would like to acknowledge my thanks and appreciation to all that have provided guidance, insight and support in the development of the Business Plan Workbook.

In particular I would like to acknowledge my thanks and appreciation to Northeastern University for providing me the opportunity to be involved with such a great organization and so many wonderful colleagues.

I would also like to thank everyone in the Entrepreneurship & Innovation group that has provided support. To Marc Meyer for his support to me personally and to John Friar for all of his advice and input keeping everything in the right perspective.

I would like to thank all the students through the years for their willingness to provide feedback about the Workbook and for what they taught me.

I would also like to thank Charlotte for her never ending support and for all the things she does.

About the Author

Edmund Clark is an Executive Professor at the Northeastern University, D'Amore-McKim School of Business in the Entrepreneurship and Innovation Group. As an educator he developed and teaches a Capstone business course and has taught hundreds of students and business owners to write Business Plans.

The D'Amore-McKim School of Business - Ranked #25 Undergraduate Program in the US (Business Week 2013) and #10 College for Entrepreneurship Programs (Princeton Review 2013)

ISBN 978-0-9913192-0-6

"This publication is designed to provide accurate and authoritative information in regard to the subject matter covered. It is sold with the understanding that the publisher is not engaged in rendering legal, accounting, or other professional service. If legal advice or other expert assistance is required, the services of a competent professional person should be sought."

The Business Workbook
43 Glen Ave
Upton, MA 01568
TheBusinessPlanWorkbook.com

Table of Contents

About This Book

"The Business Plan Workbook for an Owner-Managed Business" is a workbook to assist in the development of a Business Plan.

"The Business Plan Workbook" follows the format of a standard business plan and provides the user a series of worksheets to assist in the development of a business plan.

This book is unique as that it maintains a focus solely on that of an Owner-Managed business.

Each section of the business plan is presented in order, and the worksheets provide a set of questions for the reader to consider as they develop their business plan.

There are two intended users for this workbook. The first group of users of this book is students of business and potential business owners that are not experienced in the development of a new business or business plan.

For this audience, *The Business Plan Workbook* is designed to be a companion guide to the book, *"Strategy and Business Development* for an Owner-Managed Business"

"Strategy and Business Development for an Owner-Managed Business" provides insight and detail to the development of an owner managed business and guides in the development of a business plan.

The second audience of this workbook is a business owner that has business experience and an understanding of marketing, operations, accounting, and finance. For this group, *The Workbook* is intended to be used as a standalone set of worksheets to guide in the development of a business plan for strategic or financing purposes.

Chapter 1 An Introduction to Business Plans

An Introduction to Business Plans

Why Write a Business Plan?

Really, Why Write a Business Plan?

Who Do You Want to Read Your Business Plan?

Format of a Business Plan

The Key to Writing an Effective Business Plan

Guidelines for Writing a Business Plan

Principles for Writing a Business Plan

THE
BUSINESS PLAN
WORKBOOK

Chapter 1

An Introduction to Business Plans

A business plan is simply a document that describes and details key aspects about a business, including its operations, marketing and sales, products, customers, and finances.

Business Plans can take on many different styles and formats, but generally, they have four main sections: an Introduction, a Description of the Business, Financial Statements, and Supporting Documents/Appendix.

1. The **Introduction** section of the plan provides basic information for the reader. It should introduce the writer of the Business Plan to the reader, and provide insight to the reader as to why the plan was written.

2. The **Description of the Business** provides information and details about the company, its products, customers, competitors, marketing and sales, and operations. Essentially, the Description of the Business tells the reader what the business does and how it does it.

3. The **Financial Statements** section provides insight into the financial performance and health of the company. Generally, standard financial statements are provided, including an Income Statement, a Cash flow Statement, a Statement of Shareholders' Equity, and a Balance Sheet.

4. The **Supporting Documents/Appendix** section is used to provide backup documentation and references to support the Description of the Business, and the Financial Statements section.

> A Business Plan is a document that demonstrates the ability of your business to sell enough of its product or service to make a satisfactory profit and to be attractive to you or others that read the plan.

What does this definition tell us? This definition tells us that a Business Plan is a document that first and foremost demonstrates that the business makes a satisfactory profit. Not just a profit, but a satisfactory profit. Second, the document tells us that the business is attractive, to you or others that read the plan.

How does a Business Plan accomplish these two seemingly simple objectives? First it needs to demonstrate that the business is sound; that the fundamental structure and strategy of the business works. The Plan needs to clearly articulate how the business works and how the business makes money.

Second, the Business Plan needs to show the reader that the business is attractive. To do this, you need to know who the reader will be and understand what it is the reader finds to be relevant and attractive. Then, the Business Plan must clearly articulate that the business meets the reader's needs and requirements.

Why Write a Business Plan?

There are many reasons to write a Business Plan, including to prove that the business idea is feasible; to obtain funding; to attract vendors or suppliers; to implement a merger or an acquisition. You might write a business plan to explain how the business works, to attract key employees to develop operating systems, or for use in developing a franchise system.

Why Write a Business Plan?

To sell yourself on the business
To obtain bank financing
To obtain investment funds
To arrange strategic alliances
To obtain large contracts
To attract key employees
To complete mergers and acquisitions
To motivate and focus the management team

There are many reasons for a Business Plan, but when you boil them all down, it's because you need something. These needs fall into four basic categories.

Viability

The first reason to write a business plan is to determine if the business idea is viable. After you come up with some great idea, a Business Plan is a means to do your due diligence and you need to see if the idea will work as a business. Many seemingly great ideas are found to not be viable business concepts upon greater review.

Four basic reasons for writing a Business Plan:
- to determine the viability of a business
- to identify whether you are interested in pursuing the opportunity
- to use it as an operating guide
- to use it to acquire financing

Next Steps

After you realize that a business concept is viable, you may use the Business Plan process to determine if you want to pursue the idea further. As you write the Business Plan, you may find that while it is a great idea and a feasible one, for some reason it is not right for you.

Operating Guide

Another basic reason for writing a Business Plan is to develop greater insight into the business and to have a complete and thorough knowledge of how the business operates. Business Plans, when written as operating guides provide detail into the business operations. These Plans are typically more technical in nature and focus on the operations of the business.

Funding

The final, and perhaps most common, need for writing a Business Plan is to acquire funding. Business Plans are often required by banks and requested by investors to prove the validity of the business model and the ability of the management.

Really, Why Write a Business Plan?

To better understand why you should write a Business Plan, you need to understand two things. First, the truth is that a Business Plan by itself is not all that important or valuable. The value is not in the Business Plan as a document, but in knowledge and insight gained while writing the plan. The document is not the objective but rather a means to an end.

Consider the wisdom from the following quotes:

"Plans are of little importance, but planning is essential."
Winston Churchill

"Plans are nothing; planning is everything."
General Dwight D. Eisenhower

The value lies in the process of researching, analyzing and writing the Business Plan. And the reason for taking the time to do this is to minimize risk, both personal and professional, and to increase the likelihood of success.

Second, you don't have to have a Business Plan. The reality is that not all business owners write Business Plans. There are lots of business owners running successful and prosperous businesses that have never written a Business Plan. Further, there are many businesses with high quality Business Plans that have failed.

> **The Importance of Writing a Business Plan:**
> - to minimize risk; personal and professional
> - to increase the likelihood of success

So, why go through the process and all the trouble of writing one? The answer is simple. You write a Business Plan because you want to improve your chances of success and minimize risk.

If you are starting your first lemonade stand and have little at risk, perhaps you can forego the effort of writing a Business Plan. If, on the other hand, you are about to quit your job, sell your house, and mortgage the family farm, then it is a very smart idea to take some time to research what you are doing and to write a Business Plan. Writing a Business Plan is about reducing risk.

The more you have at risk, the greater the value of planning.

Who Do You Want to Read Your Business Plan?

Who you want to read your Business Plan all depends on why you wrote it. Generally, you write a Business Plan because you need something. Therefore, the person that you want most to read your plan is a person that can provide you with whatever it is that you need. For example, if you need a bank loan, then you want a banker to read it. If you are looking for equity funding, then you want an investor to read your Business Plan. The key to determining who you want to read the plan is to know what you need, and identify who it is that can give it to you.

> **Two Basic Questions**
>
> Before writing a business plan you need to answer two questions,
>
> 1. **What is the purpose of the plan?**
> 2. **Who is the intended audience?**

Two questions to ask yourself as you write your Business Plan are: What is the purpose of the plan? (What do you need?), and Who is the audience? (Who has what you need?) These are important questions to consider as you are writing because you must make sure to provide the information that the reader needs to see. Clearly understanding what you want and what the reader needs are critical to helping you get what you want from your plan.

> **Consider These Questions:**
>
> **What is the purpose of the plan?**
> • What specifically do you need?
> • Who can supply you with what you need?
> **Who is the intended audience?**
> • Who do you want to read your business plan?
> • Why would they want to read it?
> • What do they need/want to know?
> • What do you want them to know

To keep on track as you are writing, consider some additional questions, including: Why would your target reader want to read your plan? What do they need/want to know? What do you want them to know? The more you can tailor your plan to your intended audience, the more likely you will keep them interested you're your business.

Again, to determine who you want to read the plan ask yourself, "What do you need?" Be specific. Then you can ask, "Who can supply it?" Answer that, and you know who you want to read your Business Plan.

While these two questions – what do you need and who can supply it – seem simple enough, they are two deceptively difficult questions to answer. The problem is you often don't know what you need until you've invested significant effort into writing the plan.

Format of a Business Plan

There is no one universally agreed upon format for a Business Plan. However, there is basic information that is generally included in a plan regardless of the format. A basic Business Plan should include: an Introduction; Description of the Business; Financial Documentation; and Supporting Documents /Appendix.

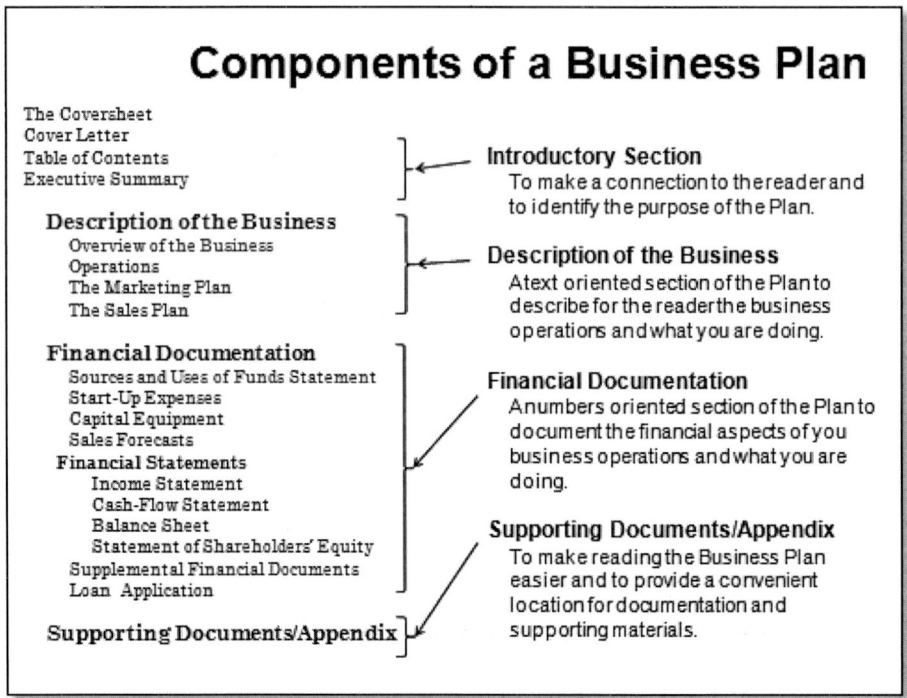

The Cover Sheet protects and binds the business plan and provides basic company and contact information.

The Introductory Section should include basic contact information and introduce the writer to the reader. As part of the introduction, include a Cover Letter, a Table of Contents, and an Executive Summary.

The Cover Letter is used to introduce the writer to the reader, and articulates why the Business Plan was written and submitted to the reader. This lets the reader know about you and what it is that you want.

The Table of Contents provides an overview of the material included and a reference to its location within the plan. This gives the reader the ability to quickly and easily find what it is that they want to read.

The Executive Summary is a critical piece of a Business Plan and the most important part. The Executive Summary provides an overview of the key information about the business and the opportunity. This section needs to answer the reader's most fundamental question and create an interest in the business opportunity.

The Description of the Business provides the reader with relevant details about the business, the opportunity, and includes details about the Operations, Marketing, and Sales of the business. This section answers the reader's questions and provides information about the business. The Description of the Business should also provide a clear explanation about the financial section that follows.

The Financial Documentation section provides the reader with relevant details regarding the financial performance and health of the business. Financial documentation is typically provided in a standardized financial format and includes an Income Statement, a Cash-Flow Statement, a Balance Sheet, and a Statement of Shareholders' Equity. Additional financial information may include performance ratios or a break-even analysis, and/or a loan application if necessary.

The Appendix and Supporting Documents section includes reference material and documentation to support the Description of the Business and the Financial Documentation. This section is used to provide the reader with additional materials in a convenient location.

If you are working with a particular bank, ask them if they have a business plan template that they would like you to use. The goal is to make their life easier with a format that they find comfortable. If your bank has a preferred format, use it.

The Key to Writing an Effective Business Plan

A good business plan is written to accomplish an objective, and this often requires someone else to read the plan. To accomplish your objective, you must write a plan that is worth reading and provides the level of detail the reader needs to support you. To get them to read your plan, whatever it is you have written must interest them; not you, them.

> ## Write to the Reader
>
> *The number 1 principle.*
> **Write to the Reader**
>   Always consider the reader's perspective.
>   Always consider:
>   • who will be reading the plan
>   • why they are reading it
>   • what is it they need to know?
>
> **Focus on answering the reader's questions.**

The key then to writing a good Business Plan is to, *"Write to the reader."* If you want someone to read your plan then focus on what they find to be interesting. For example, to write a Business Plan that a banker finds interesting, you need to focus in on what they want to know. So how do you do this? First, you must know what you need, and then you must know who it is that could help you get it. Then you consider the reader's perspective and address the issues of concern to them.

The key then to writing an effective Business Plan is to address the needs of the reader. If you focus on the needs of the reader and address their concerns, then you increase the likelihood that they will read your plan. If you do not, the chances of them reading your plan are significantly reduced. If writing an effective Business Plan means that you get your bank loan, then you've got to get a banker to read it. They will only read if what you are telling them meets their needs. If you don't meet their needs they will not read it.

It's worth repeating, the key to writing an effective Business Plan; *"Write to the reader."*

Guidelines for Writing a Business Plan

Writing a Business Plan can be time consuming. There are many moving parts to a Business Plan, and for the uninitiated, writing one can appear to be a daunting task. The good news is that writing a Business Plan it is not an insurmountable task and there are ways to make it easier.

> **Guidelines for Writing a Business Plan**
> **Process**: the process and mechanics of writing a Business Plan
> **Content**: the information necessary to accomplish your objectives
> **Principles**: principles to follow when writing a Business Plan

Before we start writing a Business Plan, let's consider the process of what we are going to do as we write our Business Plan; the content of what it is that we want to say; and identify some principles that we can follow to make the task easier.

Process

The Process of what you are going to do refers to the mechanics, or tasks associated with writing a Business Plan. Some common questions often associated with the process of writing a Business Plan include: What do you do?, Where do you start?, What do you say?, and How long should it be?

What do you do? Essentially, writing a Business Plan is an iterative process of asking and answering questions. It's a simple process; you ask questions and then answer them. The idea here is that by asking questions you will discover new information, ideas, and insights. Often, with the discovery of information comes new insights and new questions. New insights often raise new questions regarding the validity of old answers. Old answers must again be reexamined based on new insights.

> **Common Process Questions**
> • What do you do?
> • Where do you start?
> • What do you say?
> • How long should a business plan be?

Asking and answering questions is easy. The hard part is asking the right questions and not necessarily being content with easy answers just because we want to be finished. This is the hard part because we must challenge our own ideas and wisdom, or the ideas and wisdom of others. We often have to admit we don't have the answers and we need to push ourselves to find them. This is the hard part, because often we don't even know the questions we should ask. The process of asking and answering questions continues until you feel comfortable that you have answered the hard questions that need to be addressed.

It is this discovery process part of writing a Business Plan that makes the whole effort worthwhile. Discovery is an important reason to write a Business Plan. It is so important it deserves repeating; it is the discovery process of information and acquisition of knowledge part of writing a Business Plan that makes the whole effort worthwhile. This is our opportunity to acquire knowledge and craft a winning plan.

This iterative, circular process of asking and answering questions serves two functions. First, through the process of asking questions we educate ourselves and determine how we can best build a profitable business. Conversely, it is through this process that we determine the business we are investigating is

> **Writing a Business Plan Is About Answering Questions**
> - First, your questions.
> - Second, the *reader's* questions.
>
> Writing a Business Plan is not just about answering questions however; it's about answering the right questions, with the right answers.

something we decide that we do not wish to pursue for whatever reason. Perhaps it is not a profitable business, or it requires resources beyond our means of acquisition, or perhaps we just do not like the business for personal reasons.

Second, through this process we identify the relevant issues and answers to the questions that the ultimate reader of our plan will most likely ask us. Through the discovery process, we learn what we need to know to become successful in our venture. This process of discovery is the hard part.

> **Writing a Business Plan is a Process of Discovery**
> Writing a Business Plan is a process of asking and answering questions. As you ask and answer questions you learn; as you learn you ask new questions. New information often requires changes in the plan.

Perhaps the hardest part of the discovery process is identifying what the right questions are that need to be asked. Answering questions is easy. Answering the right questions requires effort.

Where do you start when writing a Business Plan? There is no single right place to start when writing a Business Plan. That being said, a good place to begin is with a standard template of a Business Plan. A standard template gives you a format to follow and makes the writing process easier for you. A template serves as a guide for you to make certain that you include all the necessary information and materials. Breaking down the Business Plan into pieces makes the process of writing it more manageable and less intimidating. Also, if you start with a format the reader is familiar with, your reader will find the final product to be more comfortable.

When working with a template, you can start writing anywhere in the template that you choose. Fill in any section you can. Fill in the easy sections. Answer the questions that you can answer that need to be answered. Start with taking the easy road by answering easy questions until you realize that you need additional information. This is where the heavy lifting starts. When you can no longer answer the easy questions, or when you realize you need better information to answer them properly, you need to research the questions and discover the answers.

When you are writing a Business Plan, it's a question of what comes first, the chicken or the egg. The good news for us is that we don't need to answer that question. Start wherever you feel comfortable and work your way around the plan template. Writing a Business Plan is an iterative and circular exercise. This is because you often need to repeat and return to prior material. So it doesn't really matter where you start, you will most likely end up returning to verify, confirm or change exiting materials. You keep going around and around, adjusting and adding material until you feel your Business Plan is complete.

One recommended process to follow when writing a Business Plan is to start with the **Business Concept Development** worksheets to help you quickly develop an overview of the business. Roughly estimate the scope of the business for sales, operations and marketing. Now with a rough idea of the size and scope of the business, continue to develop sales estimates, operations and marketing. First, develop more finely-tuned sales estimates. With clear sales goals estimates you can then begin to develop the operations necessary to achieve those sales goals. Then you can develop a marketing mix to promote and sell your products.

What do you say? What you say depends on two questions; why you are writing the Business Plan, and who do you want to read it? While those seem like two simple questions, they can be deceptively difficult to answer. It is important though to answer those questions as honestly as possible as they drive the entire process of writing your plan.

The first question, Why do you want to write a Business Plan?, seems simple enough. You write a Business Plan because you need something. The problem, however, is that often you don't really know what you need until you put in a great deal of effort writing the plan.

The answer to the second question, who do you want to read your Business Plan, also seems simple enough. You want the person to read your Business

Plan to be someone that can give you what you need. With this in mind, everything you say in the plan should be focused on this objective.

So what do you say? Tell the reader the things that are important to them. You don't need to tell the reader everything; only what they want and need to know. For each of the summary sections, **Overview of the Business**, **Operations**, **Marketing**, and **Sales Plans** discuss the most important points included in the subsections that follow. In each subsequent section, discuss the main issues in greater detail. So what's important? It depends. It depends on the business and what you are doing and what you need.

How long should a business plan be? No longer than necessary. As always, you should think about the plan from the reader's perspective. What do they need to know, and what could you reasonably expect them to read? A one-page Business Plan is most likely not going to provide enough information, and three hundred pages would be too much to expect someone to read. What it boils down to is how quickly can you tell them what they need and want to know, and what is reasonable to expect them to read.

For an average small business applying for a bank loan, you could reasonably expect the Description of the Business to be anywhere between 10 to 30 pages. Less than 10 most likely does not convey enough information, and more than 30 pages would be unreasonable to expect someone to read.

Thirty pages might sound like a lot, but it really is not. Remember there are four main summary sections, **Overview of the Business**, **Operations**, **Marketing**, and **Sales Plans** and 18 or so subsections depending on your business. This means that you need to write roughly one page per section. Not every section needs to be a page and some likely need to be longer. Some sections may only be a paragraph or two; it really depends on what you need to tell the reader. If you are doing a good job researching your business, you will have volumes of information and what you will find is that you are working hard to edit information out of the plan to make it shorter.

Considering that you only have a page or less per section, get to the important issues quickly. You really only have enough space to discuss two, three or perhaps four things. So, discuss the three or four things that really matter. What are they? It depends on what you need and whom you need to get it from. For example, you generally borrow money for one of two reasons. You borrow money to either acquire revenue-generating assets or to cover negative, short-term cash flow operational expenses. So if you are borrowing money to acquire capital equipment, then you must go into detail about the equipment that you are buying in the operations section and then discuss how it will make money to pay back the loan.

Principles for Writing a Business Plan

Writing a good Business Plan is part art, and part science. The science portion requires that some level of formula be followed and that validation and references support theories and assumptions. The art of writing a Business Plan is more difficult to explain. As far as what makes for a good Business Plan, it's difficult to say, but to paraphrase United States Supreme Court Justice Potter Stewart, "*I know it when I see it*".

The C's of Writing a Business Plan:

• Content
• Connected
• Clear
• Concise
• Compelling
• Consistent

So how do we create a good business plan? Mix science with art. For the science, follow a formula and validate your assumptions. For the art, follow some generally accepted principles. First and foremost, "Write to the Reader". Second, consider the C's of Writing a Business Plan: Content, Connected, Clear, Concise, Compelling, and Consistent

Content

A Business Plan should provide the information and content that the reader needs to make an informed decision and take action.

Write to the Reader: Answer the Reader's Questions
Understand the reader's perspective and their needs, and tell them what they want to know. To them, what they want to know is what's compelling.

A Banker Has Five Basic Questions
How much money do you need?	(*Amount*)
What are you going to do with the money?	(*Purpose*)
When do you need it & for how long?	(*Timing*)
How will you pay me back?	(*Capacity*)
How can you assure me that I will get my money back?	(*Collateral*)

Provide Facts
Opinions and Assumptions are Not Facts. If you cannot or do not document it with verifiable facts, it's an opinion.

The Reader's Opinion Is Always Right
When you want something from the reader, if there is a difference of opinion between the two of you, you are wrong.

Communicate Strategy
A Business Plan communicates the strategy of the business and how/why it will be successful. Show the reader the strategy that you have crafted and how it will result in a viable and profitable business.

Some Things Are Important
Identify what's important (to the reader) and discuss it.

Detail the Important
If it's important, provide detail. The devil is in the details.

Ignore the Unimportant
If it's not important (to the reader), don't include it. Knowing what to leave out is as important as knowing what to put in.

Don't Give the Reader Information They Don't Need
If the reader doesn't need something, don't include it. Including information that is not needed can confuse or distract the reader or raise new questions that you don't need or want to address.

Create Confidence
The content of your Business Plan should instill confidence in the reader that you know what you are doing. The plan needs to make the reader confident that it will work and that you have the skills and abilities to execute the plan.

Business Plans are Substantive
Develop substance to your ideas and your answers.
- No *Fluff*
- Provide documented facts

Don't Raise Questions Unless You Answer Them
A Business Plan is not the place for rhetorical questions; it's a place for answers.

Don't Raise Questions You Don't Want to Answer

Sometimes you're better off not answering questions. Be careful, however, that the reader doesn't think that you are trying to hide inconvenient information.

A Business Plan is Not a Book Report
Business Plans answer questions and express a strategy.

Consider the Five W's and an H
Answer the readers' questions as they relate to the: who, what, why, where, when, and how of your business.
Provide details for your **business** as to:
- What you are doing?
- Where you are doing it?
- When you are doing it?
- How you are doing it?
- Why you are doing it?
- Who are you?

Connected

Every activity within a business is interconnected and affects the rest of the business. All the tactics and actions discussed in the business plan, within each section should complement each other.

Connect the Dots
Everything in the plan must be connected. The text and the financials are interrelated. The text explains the numbers, and the numbers align with the text. Everything is connected.

Connect Strategy
When you have a strategic plan for marketing, for example a high price, it must be reflected in all aspects of your business, including the product, production, customer service, etc.

Clear

A plan should be clear in content, presentation, and format. It should state clearly who you are, what you want from the reader, what the benefits are for the reader, what you are doing, how you are going to do it.

Make the Plan Clear and Easy to Read

The reader is doing you a favor; make the plan clear and easy to read. If you make it difficult for them to read it; they won't.

Use an Appropriate Business Plan Format and Standard Financial Statements
- Use a format that is standard for the reader and for the purpose of the plan.
- Provide the information the reader needs in a clear and logical format.

Label, List, and Describe
This is part of making the plan clear and easy to read.

Document, Footnote, and Explain
Again, part of making the plan clear and easy to read.

Tell the Reader the Conclusion
Do not expect a reader to come to your or any other particular conclusion. If you want the reader to come to a conclusion, tell them up front what the point is, and then drive them to it.

Use Facts to Make Your Case
Opinions are not facts. Facts can be documented and proven; opinions cannot. Opinions don't count. *The man without facts has only an opinion.*

Substantiate Facts
Substantiate key and important facts. Be prepared to substantiate other facts.

Be specific
Be specific in what you are saying.

Use Words That Have Meaning
- Use words and phrases that quantify
- Fifty percent means something; significant means nothing.
- Words like significant, overwhelming, and superior invite questions. For example, using the word significant invites the question "Just then how significant? 50%, 100%, 10,000%? If you mean 50 percent, then say 50 percent.

State Your Assumptions
State how you arrived at your assumptions.

Provide Explanations

Do not assume the reader will see what you see. Charts, graphs, and financials are powerful but they require an explanation. What the reader interprets from a chart, etc., may not be what you want them to see.

Financials Require an Explanation

Numbers are meaningless without an explanation. You don't need to explain the math but you need to explain where the numbers come from. Pro forma Financial Statements without assumptions stated and explanations are meaningless.

Say What You Mean, Mean What You Say

The reader should not have to interpret or decipher what it is that you are trying to say. Be clear. Say what you mean.

Don't hedge Might and will are two different words. Saying you might do something is different than saying you will do something.

You Are Either Going to Do Something; Or You Are Not

- If you are going to do something; discuss it.
- If you're not or only thinking about doing it; don't discuss it.

Concise

Be concise. Tell the reader what they want to know – what they need to know – and do it quickly. Don't make the plan longer than necessary. Consider it as if every word that you write has a cost.

Get to the point

Don't Waste the Reader's Time

If it's important; discuss it. If it's not; don't.

Don't make the plan longer than necessary

Compelling

Make the content of the plan compelling, from the reader's perspective. It's not about what's in it for you that's important, but what's in it for them. Show the reader the opportunity and how they will benefit: that's what makes the plan compelling.

Answer the Reader's Questions
Understand the reader's perspective and their desires, and tell them what they want to know. What they want to know is what's compelling.

Answer the Reader's Questions Before They Are Asked
Answering questions before they are asked show the reader that you understand what is important to them.

For the Banker, It's All About the Five Basic Questions
If you need money from the bank, you must address their concerns.

Make the Plan Fun to Read
Make the plan fun to read and the reader will. How do you make it fun? You can't, and you're not expected to. Just don't make it difficult.

Consistent

The plan needs to be consistent from start to finish. There are many moving parts in a Business Plan and they must all be in alignment for it to work properly. The plan must be in alignment from the beginning to the end, from the marketing plan, to personnel, investments, operations, plant and equipment —right through to the financials.

Watch for Consistency
- Consistency in your numbers
- Consistency in your text
- Consistency between your numbers and your text

Chapter 2 Business Concept Development Worksheets

Business Concept Development Worksheets

Overview of the Business

Define Your Business Model

Environmental Trends

Financial Estimates

Customers

Competitors

Company – Operations

Company - The Marketing Plan

Chapter 2

Business Concept Development Worksheets

The Business Concept Development Worksheets are intended to help you to quickly develop a general overview of the business idea and to assess the size and potential for the business.

The worksheets can be used as a rough draft to begin the development of your Business Plan or they can be used as a first iteration of the Business Plan.

The questions included in the **Business Concept Development Worksheets** will also be address again in greater detail as you develop your Business Plan

Addressing all the questions is important, however accuracy and specifics are not the key output expected when developing and completing this assignment successfully.

Business Concept Development Worksheets

1. Overview of the Business

2. Define Your Business Model

3. Environmental Trends

4. Financial Estimates

5. Customers

6. Competitors

7. Company - Operations

8. Company - The Marketing Plan

Business Concept Development Worksheet

Overview of the Business
Page 1 of 8

Business name   Date:

Address
C S Z
Phone number
Email address
Business URL

Team Members

_____

_____

_____

Business Concept Development Worksheet

Define Your Business Model
Page 2 of 8

Describe **your Business Model**
- (What does your business do and how does it do it?)

Describe your **products/services**:
- (What do you sell?)

Who are your **customers**?

Why do they buy your products?
- (What are the **benefits** they receive?)

How do you create **Value**?
- (How do you generate revenue and profit?)

Business Concept Development Worksheet

Environmental Trends
Page 3 of 8

How large is the market for your product?

How competitive is the market?

What customer trends do you see?

What opportunities do you see in the industry? Trends?

What threats do you see in this opportunity? Trends?

Business Concept Development Worksheet

Financial Estimates
Page 4 of 8

Revenue

What do you estimate as total **sales** revenue for your business?

less than	$100,000		
between	$100,000	and	$500,000
between	$1,000,000	and	$5,000,000
between	$5,000,000	and	$10,000,000
between	$10,000,000	and	$50,000,000
over	$50,000,000		

What do you estimate as the **average sale in dollars per customer?**

less than	$5		
between	$5	and	$10
between	$10	and	$15
between	$15	and	$20
between	$_____	and	$_____

What is the **relative size** of your business?

    small   mid-sized   large

Financial resource requirements

How much money do you have to invest
in this business? $ _____

How much money do you need to borrow? $ _____

   for Start-Up Expenses $ _____

   for Capital Equipment $ _____

   for year one of Operating expenses $ _____

   Where will you get this money?   Debt   Equity

Business Concept Development Worksheet

Customers
Page 5 of 8

Describe the basic characteristics of your **customers**:

Why do they buy the types of products you (and your competitors) sell? What are the **product benefits** that the customer desires?

Purchase frequency: How often does an "average" customer buy your products?

Only once
daily
weekly
monthly
quarterly
annually

Business Concept Development Worksheet

Competitors
Page 6 of 8

On what product attributes does your product compete?
  convenience
  quality
  style
  price
  other (describe)

How do your competitors compare to you on relative size

    most are: smaller
                     larger
                     about the same size

                     franchises
                     national corporations
                     independent companies

What advantages do your competitors have over you?

What advantages do you have over your competitors?

What are the benefits of your competitor's products?

Business Concept Development Worksheet

Company – Operations
Page 7 of 8

Describe the key pieces of **technology and equipment** necessary to operate your business:

Estimate the **cost** to acquire this equipment:

Describe the facilities necessary to operate your business: (production, storage, sales requirements).

Describe the **layout** of your business: (production, storage, sales requirements). (Include a drawing if necessary)

Estimate the employee requirements to operate your business:

	Quantity	Annual Cost
Management	_____	$_____
Production personnel	_____	$_____
Sales personnel	_____	$_____

Estimate maximum **capacity** output for your Business Operations. Identify Capacity constraints.

What is your **geographical profile**:
local
regional
national
international

Business Concept Development Worksheet

Company - The Marketing Plan
Page 8 of 8

Describe your **product/services**:

What are the **benefits** customers receive from your products?

What are the **prices** for your products?

    How does your pricing compare to your competitors?
        lower
        average
        higher

    Why have you chosen this pricing structure?

How do you plan on **advertising** your products? **(Promotion)**

    What is your estimated advertising budget in dollars?
    $_____ per year

How will you **distribute** your products? (**Place**)

    How do your customers acquire your products? e.g. your location, convenience store, a website.

Describe the **sales** activities of your business

    How will you get products into the hands of your customers?

Chapter 3   Business Plan Worksheets

Some Comments about Worksheets

Business Plan Worksheets

The Coversheet

The Cover Letter

Table of Contents

The Executive Summary

Overview of the Business

Operations

The Marketing Plan

Financial Documentation

Financial Statements

Supplemental Financial Documents

Supporting Documents/Appendix

THE
BUSINESS PLAN
WORKBOOK

Chapter 3

Some Comments about Worksheets

The purpose of the worksheets is to help *guide* the development of your Business Plan. The worksheets are intended to prompt questions and guide you in the process of asking and answering questions.

Answering all the questions does not mean that you have written a good or complete business plan. Situations and businesses are different, and as such, the questions that need to be answered vary.

The goal when completing the worksheets is *not* to answer all the questions. The goal is to answer the *right* questions that provide the insight necessary for the development of a strategy and a Business Plan that will result in a successful business. The trick is to ask and answer the right questions.

Additionally, these worksheets are not intended to be a definitive resource, nor do they provide a definitive list of questions. You may find that given your situation, there are more pressing issues and questions that should be addressed.

As you move through the worksheets, expect to encounter questions for which you do not have answers. Some questions will require research to be answered and others will be found to be contingent on parts of the Business Plan for which you may not have the answers yet.

Research the question for which you need information and answer the other questions with "contingent" answers based on assumptions or best guesses at the time. As you move forward, remember that some of the answers to questions need to be reassessed and reviewed for accuracy.

Completed worksheets should be viewed as works in progress. As you progress through the development of your Business Plan you should expect to go back and review prior worksheets and add new information as it is uncovered, change outdated information, and question and re-question prior assumptions.

Business Plans are not typically written in the order in which they are presented. Nor are they generally read in the order in which they are presented. For example, typically one of if not the first things read is the Executive Summary and typically it is one of, if not the last things written.

Business Plan Worksheets

The Coversheet
Cover Letter
Executive Summary
Overview of the Business
    Industry
    Company
    Customers
    Competitors
Operations
    Technology and Equipment
    Facilities and Layout
    Management Profile
    Personnel Profile
The Marketing Plan
    Competition
    Customers
    Service/Product
    Pricing
    Promotion
    Distribution/Location and Facilities
The Sales Plan
    The Sales Team
    Sales Management
    Sales Policies
    Sales Projections
Financial Statements
    Income Statement
    Cash-Flow Statement
    Balance Sheet
    Statement of Shareholders' Equity
Supplemental Financial Documents
    Sources and Uses of Funds Statement
    Capital Equipment
    Start Up Costs (One Time Expenses)
    Sales Estimates
    Inventory
    Wages/Salaries
    Marketing - Promotional Expenses
    Loan Repayments Schedule
    Depreciation Schedule
    Loan Application
    Term Sheet
Supporting Documents/Appendix

The Coversheet

A cover sheet is an important component of a Business Plan, and every business plan needs a cover. The coversheet provides three essential purposes.

In no particular order of importance, the coversheet:
- Creates a clean, professional and attractive package
- Protects and binds the business plan
- Conveniently provides contact information for the reader so that they can quickly and easily contact you

The format is not critical as long as it looks appropriate, professionally done, is easy to read, and has the basic necessary contact information. If you have a logo, a graphic or a photograph of the business, include it on the cover. Make it look nice, as with anything; first impressions count. You need to look the part.

The Coversheet
Worksheet

Date: _____

Name: _____

Business: _____

A cover sheet is an important component of a Business Plan, and every business plan needs a cover. The format is not critical as long as it looks appropriate, professionally done, is easy to read, and has the basic necessary contact information.

If you have a logo, a graphic or a photograph of the business, include it on the cover.

Business Information:
    Business Name
    Address
    City, State Zip
    Phone
    Email
    Website

Contact Information:
    Your Name (all principals)
    Address
    City, State Zip
    Phone(s)
    Email(s)

    Date

The Cover Letter

The Cover Letter is used to introduce the writer(s) to the reader; to thank the reader for taking time to read your business plan; to articulate why the business plan was written and submitted to the reader; and to state the desired action requested from the reader.

Cover Letter
- Introduce the writer to the reader
- thank the reader for taking time to read your business plan
- Articulate why the business plan was written and submitted to the reader
- State the desired action requested from the reader upon completion of reading the business plan
- Qualify the opportunity between the reader and the writer

The Cover Letter should ideally be one page in length, but no more than two pages. The Cover Letter is used to tell the reader who you are, what you want, and what you want from them. The Cover Letter should be direct, explicit and to the point. State specifically and directly; "This is what I need. This is what I want from you."

The cover letter is most likely the first section of a business plan that the banker will read; even before the executive summary. To keep the interest of the banker you must get to the point and answer their most basic questions very quickly.

Questions a Banker Wants Answered in a Cover Letter
- How much money do you need?
- What are you going to do with the money?
- When do you need it & for how long?
- How will you pay me back?
- How can you assure me that I will get my money back?

The purpose of the Cover Letter is not to elaborate details of what you are doing but to briefly state the answer to basic questions; who you are and what you want. For example, when going for a loan, how much money are you asking for; what are you going to do with the money, how long you need it for, how you will repay them, and how you can assure them that you will give them their money back.

Lastly, a major objective of the Cover Letter is to "qualify" the reader. As a business person looking to structure financing for your business, you need to verify that the person you are dealing with has the ability and desire to support your financial needs. You are essentially trying to determine if they are the right person to be speaking with, in other words are they "ready, willing, and able" to support you. To qualify the reader, be direct in stating exactly what you want from them.

The Cover Letter
Worksheet

Date: _____
Name: _____
Business: _____

Issues to consider:

- Identify who you are.
- Articulate why the business plan was written and submitted to the reader.
- State the desired action requested from the reader.
- Qualify the opportunity between the reader and the writer

For example:
Address the reader's (a banker's) issues:

- How much money is being requested?
- What are you going to do with the money?
- How long do you need it for?
- How the funds will be repaid?
- How can you assure me that I will get my money back?

For example:
Address the reader's (an investor's) issues:

- How much money is being requested?
- What are you going to do with the money?
- What is the equity percentage being offered
- What is the valuation of the business?
- What revenue does the business achieve?
- How will we achieve an equity event?

Table of Contents

For the reader, the TOC's first function is to provide an overview of the material included. The Table of Contents provides the reader a reference to quickly locate the information and material included in the plan.

> **Table of Contents**
> - Provides an overview of the material included
> - Provides the reader with a reference of the material included in the plan and its location
> - Identifies the structure of the plan
> - Provides the writer with a template to develop the plan

With a well-documented TOC, the reader can see what is included in the plan and where it can be found.

Business plans are not read cover-to-cover like a novel, and readers often skip around from section to section. As a reader's interest is piqued they often jump from one section to another to find greater detail, clarification or validation. Providing a well labeled TOC makes the readers job of jumping from point to point easier.

For the writer, the TOC provides a structured format to help you develop your plan. Use the table of contents as an outline to start writing your plan and add content to it as you move forward. The TOC helps to break the seemingly overwhelming task of writing a business plan into smaller more manageable pieces.

Start the process of writing your plan with a standard format Table of Contents and make adjustments to it as necessary.

EXAMPLE:
The Table of Contents

Table of Contents

The Executive Summary

For many the executive summary is considered to be the most important section of the business plan. Many experienced business plan readers say this is the first and often only section of a business plan that they read. If you don't hook the reader and capture their attention here you can lose them, and your opportunity with them, permanently. To capture their attention you have to tell them what they want to know, and quickly.

The purpose of the Executive Summary is to provide an overview of the business plan, answer the reader's initial questions, and create interest in and sell the excitement of the business.

> **The Executive Summary**
> - Provides an overview of the business plan
> - Answers the reader's (the banker's) basic questions
> - Creates interest in the reader and sells the excitement of the business

The Executive Summary should contain only the most important issues and information that the reader needs to know. The Executive Summary should contain the key information that is in the business plan and there should not be anything in the executive summary that is not fully documented in the plan. If it's not important or relevant; it's not in the Executive Summary. If it is important or relevant; it's in the executive summary.

A major task of the executive summary is to answer the reader's (a banker's) basic questions. By answering their most important questions right up front, it shows them that you know what's important; important to them. For a business looking to acquire debt financing from a lender, more specifically from a bank, the reader (the banker) generally has five basic interrelated questions.

> **Basic Questions a Banker Wants Answered When Going For a Loan**
> - How much money do you need?
> - What are you going to do with the money?
> - When do you need it and for how long?
> - How will you pay me back?
> - How can you assure me that I will get my money back?

The executive summary is typically between two to five pages long, with two being preferable.

As the Executive Summary provides the highlights of the Business Plan, it is generally one of the last things in the business plan that you write.

The Executive Summary
Worksheet

Date: _____

Name: _____

Business: _____

Provide an overview of the business
- The Industry
- Strategy
- Operations
- Marketing
- Personnel

Answer the reader's (a banker's) basic questions
- How much money do you need?
- What are you going to do with the money?
- When do you need it and for how long?
- How will you pay me back?
- How can you assure me that I will get my money back?

Additional questions to consider:
- What does your business do to make money?
- How do you market to and acquire customers? How will the funding be repaid?
- What's special about your company?
- What type of financial return will be generated from the acquired funds?
- What are your margins?
- What type of margins will the invested fund return?
- How do your margins compare to others in your industry?
- What resources do you need to be successful?
- What are the strengths and weakness of your company?
- What are the opportunities and threats for your company?
- How can you assure me that I will get my money back?

Overview of the Business

The **Overview of the Business** is intended to provide the reader with a high-level view of the Business Model, the opportunity, the industry and the environment in which the business operates.

> **Overview of the Business**
> Industry
> Company
> Customers
> Competitors

The **Overview of the Business** is a summary of the key points and information that follow in the, **Industry, Company, Customers, and Competitors** sections.

The **Overview of the Business** section is not intended to provide detail about the businesses operations, marketing or finances of the business, but rather to provide a basic understanding business, the opportunity and context for the world and industry in which the business operates.

The trick for **The Overview of the Business** section is to write an engaging high-level discussion of the business and the world in which it operates that remains relevant for the reader while not sounding like a book report. Details of

> **The Overview of the Business**
> • Provide an overview of the Business Model
> • Provide an overview of the opportunity
> • Identify the information the reader needs to know
> • Provide the framework in which you will discuss your business

what you are doing come in the following Operations, and Marketing and Sales Plans sections.

The information acquired during the Strategy Development process can be used to write The Overview of the Business section.

Use industry statistics and aggregate customer and competitor data to build evidence for your business case.

Overview of the Business Worksheet

Date: _____

Name: _____

Business: _____

Questions to consider:

Industry
- What are the most pressing environmental factors in your industry?
- What are the key customer trends?
- What are the competitive forces that drive your industry?
- What recent changes have happened lately in your industry?

Company
- What does your business do to make money?
- What products do you produce/provide?
- What products categories do you produce/provide?
- What are the key factors for success in your business?
- What are typical margins in your industry?
- What resources do you need to be successful?
- What are the opportunities and threats in this industry?

Customers (Industry Focus)
- How big is the overall market?
- What customer trends are occurring in your industry?
- What product features and benefits are customers looking for?
- What customer trends do you see in your industry?

Competitors
- How many competitors are there in your industry?
- What are the key competitive issues for business in your industry?

Overview of the Business

Industry

The Environment: defines the potential for opportunity

The factors that affect the industry in which you operate impact virtually every aspect of your business from the products you provide, to how and to whom you market and sell them, to the price and profit margins you are able to obtain, and to how competitive of an environment you will face.

The Industry section of the plan provides the reader with an understanding of the world in which you operate your business. An Industry is comprised of the groups of **customers**, **competitors** and **companies** that supply and purchase products and services for a closely related need. For example, the automotive parts industry or the printing industry. Industry is a loosely used term to describe people or companies engaged in related and interrelated commercial enterprises.

Description of the Industry
- Connect your business to the world in which you operate
- Identify opportunities in the world around you
- Identify perils and pitfalls in the world in which you operate
- Install confidence in the banker that you are aware of the issues and opportunities

---

Every industry has some broader environmental issues and trends that affect and shape the companies and customers within it.

Environmental factors include (but are not limited to):
- Economic
- Legal
- Technology
- Demographics
- Social/Cultural
- Substitute Products
- Political/Legal
- Suppliers

In this section, identify the key environmental factors that are shaping the industry in which you operate.

Overview of the Business
Industry
Worksheet

Date: _____
Name: _____
Business: _____

Questions to consider:

- What industry is your business in? Describe.
- What are the most pressing environmental factors in your industry?
  Consider all environmental factors:
    - Economic
    - Legal
    - Technology
    - Demographics
    - Social/Cultural
    - Substitute Products
    - Political/Legal
    - Suppliers
- What are the key customer trends?
- Who are the key competitors in your industry?
- What actions have major competitors taken lately?
- How competitive is your industry?
- What recent changes have happened lately in your industry?
- How has your company adapted to environmental factors?
- How has your company adapted to competitors?
- What are the opportunities and threats within your industry?

Overview of the Business

Company

Company: determined by the resources that you are able to acquire, combined with your ability to create products, acquire customers, and manage finances

The Overview of the Business, Company section is not intended to provide specific detail into the businesses operations, marketing, or finances of the business, but rather to provide a basic understanding of the Business Model and some background on the company itself.

For example, how did it start? Who started it and why? Has it changed? How? Will it change in the future? Use the Company section to provide the reader with background information and history regarding the business. For example, let the reader know if it is a sole proprietorship, partnership, or incorporated, and identify the owners and key employees. How many people does the company employ? How big is it; sales in revenue in dollars and units; market share?

> **Description of the Company**
> - Provide background information
> - Provide a discussion about the structural aspects of the business
> - Provide insight as to the culture and personality of the company

This section can be used to provide the reader with the structural aspects of your business and insight into its culture and "personality". For example, does the company have a "people" friendly culture? Are there some unique personnel policies; do you emphasize customer service, employee training or benefits?

Overview of the Business
Company
Worksheet

Date: _____

Name: _____

Business: _____

Questions to consider:

- Describe your Business Model.
- What does your business do to make money?
- What products/services do you produce/provide? Describe them.
- What are the key factors for success in your business?
- How do you market to and acquire customers?
- What's special about your company?
- What is the culture of your company?
- What type of financial return will be generated from the acquired funds?
- What are your margins?
- How do your margins compare to others in your industry?
- What are the key factors for success in your business?
- What significant resources does your company currently control?
- What resources do you need to be successful?
- Where can your company get the required resources?
- What are the strengths and weakness of your company?
- What competitive advantages does your company possess?
- What do your customers think about your company?
- What is your position compared to your competitors?
- Compared to your competitors, what is the relative size of your business?
- What is your estimated total sales revenue?
- What is your geographical footprint?
- Where/how to you distribute (sell) you product?
- What product categories do you produce/provide?
- Discuss some of the basic history and background of your business.
- Where is your business located?
- How many employees do you have?

Overview of the Business

Customers

Customers: provide a business an opportunity to transform a product into a profit

The Overview of the Business, Customers section is your opportunity to provide the reader with a broad overview of the market you sell to and why they buy from you from an industry perspective.

The **Customers** section within the **Overview of the Business** section should remain general and provide aggregate information about your company's customer base; the size of the market, growth, purchasing trends and patterns.

Customers (Segments)
- Provide an overview of your customer segments
- Identify why customers buy your products
- Identify why others do not buy from you
- Show trends and purchasing habits of your customer segments

---

This is your opportunity to discuss your customers as a group from an industry perspective.

Provide high level of information, but work to avoid having the plan sound like a statistical report. Aim to keep a broad level of information connected and relevant to your business and what you are doing.

As you progress through the plan, go from general information to more specific details and documentation.

It is important for you to be able to discuss your customer segments as groups, as it can help you to identify trends in their buying habits and changes in the market. Information in this section will be important for you when you get to promotional and advertising opportunities. As you discuss your customer segments, consider and how Environmental Factors impact them.

Overview of the Business
Customers
Worksheet

Date: _____

Name: _____

Business: _____

Questions to consider:

- How big is the overall market?
- How big is the segment of the overall market?
- How is the segment different from the overall market?
- Who are the target customers? Demographics, etc.?
- Describe the basic characteristics of your customers.
- What customer trends are occurring in your industry?
- In general terms, why do customers buy your products?
- What product features and benefits are customers looking for?
- What customer trends do you see in your industry?
- Explain the purchase frequency of your customers. How often does an "average" customer purchase your products?
- Estimate the average sale in dollars per customer.
- Other?

Overview of the Business

Competitors

Competitors: redefine your environment, your opportunity to create and sell a product, and your access to resources

The Overview of the Business, Competitors section is your opportunity to provide the reader with a broad overview of the competitors within your industry.

As you did in the Customer section, consider your competitors from an industry perspective.

> **Description of Competitors Section**
> - Provide an overview of your competitors
> - Provide key distinctions between your company and your competitors
> - Identify how you are differentiated from your competitors
> - Identify competitive advantages and

Discuss not only the competitors that fight head-to-head selling the same products, but those that are indirect competitors and vie for your customers with different or substitute products.

Overview of the Business
Competitors
Worksheet

Date: _____
Name: _____
Business: _____

Questions to consider:

- How many competitors are there in your industry?
- Who are the largest competitors in your industry?
- What advantages do you competitors in your industry have over you?
- What advantages do you have over your competitors?
- On what basis do you compete with your competitors in your industry?
- What are you doing or what can you do to beat competitors in your industry?
- Why do non-customers buy from your competitors?
- What are sales, revenue, margin trends of you and your competitors?
- What are the benefits of your competitor's products?
- What are the key competitive issues for business in your industry?
- What trends do you see with competitors in your industry?
- What is your intended position, compared to your competitors?

Operations

Operations are the activities associated with creating your products and delivering them to your customers to make money.

Operations
Technology and Equipment
Facilities and Layout
Management Profile
Personnel Profile

The **Operations** section is used to provide a high-level overview of the Business Operations including: Technology and Equipment, Facilities and Layout, Management Profile, and Personnel Profile. In this introductory section, summarize what the business does to create its products and how, and address the reader's basic questions from an Operational perspective.

- **How much money is being requested?** Are you buying equipment or looking to fund business Operations? If so, how much money do you need? Be specific, e.g., X amount for expenses, Y amount for equipment.

- **What are you going to do with the money?** Itemize amounts. Be specific, e.g., provide a list of expenses; a list of the equipment. A key question the reader wants to know here is, are the requested funds going to produce new revenues and new profits?

- **How long do you need it for?** Weeks, months, years?

- **How the funds will be repaid?** Will requested funds be paid from new revenues or existing cash flows? Will new equipment create new products and cash flow?

- **How can you assure me that I will get my money back?** If you are acquiring new assets can they be in part used as collateral? What else can you offer as an assurance of repayment?

Generally speaking, the Operations section is:
- Technical in nature,
- Specific to the type of business, and
- Directly related and connected to the financial section.

The Operations section has the potential to be connected to virtually all financial sections of the Business Plan.

Identify and list equipment to be purchased and include sources and costs.

Operations
Introduction
Worksheet

Date: _____

Name: _____

Business: _____

Technology and Equipment - Questions to consider:

- Describe the production process of your business.
- What technology and equipment do you use in your business?
- Are you borrowing money for capital equipment or technology?
  - How much money is being requested?
  - What are you going to do with the money?
  - Be specific. Provide a list and specifications.
  - How much does the equipment cost?
- Do you have any proprietary technology, equipment, process or operations?

Facilities and Layout - Questions to consider:
- Where will/is your business be located? Identify the location.
- How much space do you need?
- Discuss important Facilities and Layout issues including:
  - Layout
  - Locations
  - Etc.
- How do your facilities and layout impact your business?
- What facilities and layout requirements are necessary to operate your business?
- Are renovations/improvements required for an existing location?
  - What is required and what are the costs? Be specific. Provide a list and specifications.

Management Profile - Questions to consider:
- What is the organizational structure of the business?
- What are the key positions necessary to operate the business?
- Who are the key managers?
  - What is their experience/expertise?
  - What direct industry experience do they have?

- What key functional expertise does the business have?

Personnel Profile - Questions to consider:
- How many employees does the business need?
- When are they needed? Hours, schedules?
- What are the costs associated with personnel?
- What are the costs associated with the management of personnel?

Develop and provide supplemental spreadsheets for Operational expenses.

Identify associated:
>   **Start-up and One-time Expenses** (expenses)
>   **Capital Equipment** (costs)
>   **Operating Expenses** (expenses)

Connect supplemental statements to the appropriate financial statements.

Reference and note all associated **Operations** expenditures on the appropriate financial spreadsheets, e.g., Capital Equipment, One-time & Start-up Costs and Expenses, Income Statement, Cash Flow Statement, Balance Sheet.

Operations

Technology and Equipment

Use the **Technology and Equipment** section to identify the equipment and technology used in the operation of the business, to further your explanation of your business operation, and to discuss how technology and equipment create operation effectiveness and efficiencies in your business.

Technology and equipment are used to support your business operations and make money. Technology is pervasive in every aspect of a business's operations. Both technology and equipment are used in to make your business more effective and more efficient.

Technology and Equipment
- Identify the equipment and technology used in the operation of the business
- Further your explanation of your business operations
- Discuss how technology and equipment create operation effectiveness and efficiencies in your business

---

You should include a list of the key and major pieces of technology and equipment that you use in the business, and if relevant, explain how you use them.

You do not need to list every last piece of equipment, but you should include categories and discuss the items that are of particular importance or significance to your business.

If you own significant pieces of equipment you will want to list them and their value as they may be used as collateral.

Operations
Technology and Equipment
Worksheet

Date: _____
Name: _____
Business: _____

Technology and Equipment - Questions to consider:

- Describe the production process of your business.
- Discuss the technology and equipment that you use in your business.
- What are the key pieces of equipment and technology used in your business?
- At what percent of capacity is your business operating?
- Are you borrowing money for capital equipment or technology or equipment?
  - Provide a list and specifications, with equipment costs?
- What return will the investment provide?
- Do you have any proprietary technology, equipment, process or operations?
- Who operates your technology and equipment?
- Will employee training be required?
- How does your technology and equipment compare to that of your competitors?
- How does your level of investment in technology and equipment compare to that of your competitors?
- What raw materials and supplies do you use in your production processes?
- What are your material costs of supply including shipping, handling and storage
- Discuss the availability and quality of your supply and suppliers
- Discuss quality control
- Discuss inventory management
- Identify and list equipment, raw materials, and other costs to be purchased with supplier sources and associated costs.
- What is the Capacity capability of the equipment?
- Provide a drawing of the Provide production process details and flow charts if appropriate.

Operations

Facilities and Layout

The **Facilities and Layout** section is your opportunity to provide the reader with a discussion and visualization of the physical operations of your business.

For some businesses, this section is very important. For other businesses, this section is of little value. For example, for a retail business or for a restaurant, the Facilities and Layout are critical. Customer access, parking, and location, the layout of the operation and the decor can make or break your business.

For other types of businesses, such as many business consultants or service providers, Facilities and Layout is of little or no consequence.

Facilities and Layout
- Provide the reader with a visualization of the operations of your business
- Provides documentation of the operation of the business
- Describes the equipment and technology layout and materials process flow

---

As with everything in your Business Plan, you need to determine if it's important. If it is, you need to discuss it. If it's not important, don't to go into great detail.

For a retail store or restaurant, for example, you might want to include a layout of the facility and identify key sections such as where tables and inventory are located, and where cooking and or service stations are located. You can mention cues to the ambiance and other physical characteristics of the space but they will be discussed in greater detail in the Market section. Provide information such as square footages, lighting design, operational materials handling and flow.

For a manufacturing business, Facilities and Layout plays an important part of its physical operations. Again, you should include a layout of the facility and identify key components of the operation and how they support your business activities. Additionally, location may be relevant as it impacts access suppliers and customers.

If you are planning to make changes or upgrades to the facilities, this is the section where you should provide that information. The reader will want you to estimate costs and show potential vendors or contracts to verify expenses. Include any contracts or estimates in the Supporting Documents and Appendix section.

Operations
Facilities and Layout
Worksheet

Date: _____

Name: _____

Business: _____

Questions/issues to consider:

- Where will/is your business be located? Identify the location.
- How much space do you need?
- Discuss important Facilities and Layout issues including:
    - Layout
    - Locations
    - Access to shipping /transportation/ to highways, airports, etc.
    - Customer access and proximity
    - Availability of utilities
    - Leases/rent
    - Parking
    - Square footage
    - Zoning
    - Other services
- Identify your monthly facilities related expenses (identify & list)
    - Rent
    - Utilities
    - HVAC
    - Electricity
    - Water
    - Insurance
    - Total costs, per square foot
- Is this the best location for the operations of your business?
- How does your facilities and layout impact your business?
- What facilities and layout requirements are necessary to operate your business?
- Are renovations/improvements required to an existing location?
    - What is required and what are the costs?
    - Be specific. Provide a list and specifications.
    - What return will the investment provide?
- Provide a drawing of the facilities and operational layout if appropriate

Operations

Management Profile

The **Management Profile** section is your opportunity to provide the reader with the organizational structure of the business and a detailed background of the people that will be running it.

In this section discuss the organizational structure of the business and discuss the skills and abilities that are required to manage and operate the business. Continue your discussion with highlights of the qualifications, skills and abilities of the business owners and the management team.

Discuss the management structure and how the business will be run. Consider the management by functional areas and identify the key people and their expertise.

If appropriate, provide an organizational chart and job descriptions for each key management position. List the size of departments and include hours of operations.

Management Profile
- Discuss the organizational structure of the business
- Detail the management and operational skills of the business owners and operators
- Discuss the managerial requirements of the business
- Highlight the abilities of management

Include copies of resumes of the owners and top management in the Supporting Documents section.

If you do not have the personnel necessary to run the business at this time, discuss the types of positions and requirements of those positions that you need to fill.

Operations Management Profile Worksheet

Date: _____

Name: _____

Business: _____

Questions/issues to consider:

- What is the organizational structure of the business?
    - Provide an organizational chart
- What are the key positions necessary to operate the business?
- What management skills are necessary to operate the businesses?
- Who are the key managers?
    - What is their experience/expertise?
    - What direct industry experience do they have?
    - How is it relevant to the business?
    - What is their educational background?
- What key functional expertise does the business need?
- What key functional expertise does the business have?
    - e.g. accounting, legal, marketing
- Do you have a Board of Advisors/Directors?
    - Who are they?

Reference and note all associated **Management** expenditures on the appropriate financial spreadsheets, e.g., Capital Equipment, One-time and Start-up Costs and Expenses, Income Statement, Cash Flow Statement, Balance Sheet.

Operations

Personnel Profile

The **Personnel Profile** section is your opportunity to provide the reader with the employment requirements of the business and to highlight the skills and abilities of the people employed by the business.

Use this section to define the personnel requirements of the business, including how many employees does the business need, and when? Identify what the employees will be doing. How much will they be paid, total cost, hours of employment?

Personnel Profile
- Detail the personnel requirements of the business
- Highlight the skills and abilities of the people employed by the business
- Discuss the company's efforts to attract, hire and retain employees
- Discuss logistics of the business and employee requirements, e.g., hours of operation, number of employees, employment schedule, wages, costs, etc.

For many businesses, particularly in service industries, the cost of employees can be a major expense, and attracting, hiring, and retaining employees are key priorities for the business.

Use this section to highlight the businesses requirements for employees and, if helpful, discuss your use of employment contracts, if you have a personnel handbook and employee benefits. If you have them, and it will advance your plan, consider including samples in the appendix.

Consider employee requirements by functional areas and identify the people and their expertise. If you do not have the personnel at this point, discuss the types of positions and requirements of those positions that you need to fill. Include an organizational chart if it would help to explain the business structure.

Discuss any training that will be required and how you plan to accommodate employee training.

Include a daily/weekly or monthly Employee Schedule (see: supplemental worksheets) to show how many employees the business will have and the associated costs.

Operations
Personnel Profile
Worksheet

Date: _____

Name: _____

Business: _____

Questions/issues to consider:

- How many employees does the business need?
- When are they needed? Hours, schedules?
- What will the employees be doing?
- How much will employees be paid? Rates, wages?
- How will employees be paid? Hourly, salary, commission?
- What are your policies for attracting, hiring, and retaining employees?
- Will you have employment contracts? Non-compete agreements?
- What is the organizational structure of the business?
- What are the positions necessary to operate the business?
- What skills do employees need to be successful in their position?
- What training will the business need to provide to employees?
- What are the personnel policies of the business?
  - e.g., hiring, training, vacation, pay, advancement, firing
- What are the costs associated with personnel?
- What are the costs associated with the management of personnel?

Include a daily/weekly or monthly Employee Schedule to show how many employees the business will have and the associated costs.

Reference and note all associated **Personnel** expenditures on the appropriate financial spreadsheets, e.g., Capital Equipment, One-time and Start-up Costs and Expenses, Income Statement, Cash Flow Statement, Balance Sheet.

The Marketing Plan

The **Marketing Plan** section is your opportunity to show the reader how you plan to market and promote your products and business. The Marketing Plan itself is a compilation of the 4P's of Marketing (product, price, promotion

The Marketing Plan
Competition
Customers
Service/Product
Pricing
Promotion
Distribution/Location and Facilities

place) and how they relate to your customers and competitors. The Marketing Plan identifies how you will satisfy your customers and compete against your competitors.

In the introductory Marketing section, summarize key issues regarding what the business does to market and promote its product. Address marketing/promotion with a perspective that considers the reader's basic questions.

- **How much money is being requested?** Are you requesting money to fund marketing or promotional activities? If so, how much money do you need? Do you expect your marketing/promotion activities to drive new sales?

- **What are you going to do with the money?** Itemize amounts. Be specific, e.g., provide a list of itemized activities and timing of expenses.

- **How long do you need it for?** Weeks, months, years?

- **How the funds will be repaid?** Will requested funds be paid from new revenues or existing cash flows?

- **How can you assure me that I will get my money back?** If you are acquiring new assets can they be in part used as collateral? What else can you offer as an assurance of repayment?

Identify associated **Marketing** costs on the appropriate worksheets:
  Start-up and One-time Expenses (expenses)
  Capital Equipment (costs)
  Operating Expenses (expenses)

Connect Supplemental statements to the appropriate financial statements.

The Marketing Plan
Introduction
Worksheet

Date: _____
Name: _____
Business: _____

Competition (Direct Competitors) - Questions to consider:
- Who are your top three (top x) competitors?
- Who is your top (#1) competitor?
- How do they threaten you?
- What advantages do these competitors have over you?

Customers - Questions to consider:
- Why do your customers buy your product?
- What do they buy from you?
- What are their buying patterns?

Product/Service - Questions to consider:
- What are the products and services that you sell?
- Describe the features and benefits of your products and services
- Do you have any new product development opportunities on tap?

Pricing - Questions to consider:
- What is your pricing strategy?
- What are the goals of your pricing strategy? E.g., volume or margins?
- How does your pricing strategy align with your other marketing decisions? E.g., promotion, place, product choices.
- Do your prices create reasonable and acceptable margins? What are they?

Promotion - Questions to consider:
- How will you promote, your products and services?
- What is your Promotional Strategy (strategies)?
- What promotional tools do you use?
- What are your key promotional tactics:
- How will these promotional programs benefit your company?
- How much will each promotional campaign cost?
- Are they aligned properly?

- Are they cost effective?
- Are they efficient?
- Are these the best promotional choices? Why?

Place (Distribution/Location and Facilities) - Questions to consider:
- What is your market coverage strategy? Why?
- How will you get your product/service to your customers?
- What channels will you sell through?
- What are the key attributes of your location and facilities?

Reference and note all associated **Marketing** expenditures on the appropriate financial spreadsheets, e.g., Capital Equipment, One-time and Start-up Costs and Expenses, Income Statement, Cash Flow Statement, Balance Sheet.

The Marketing Plan

Competition

Competitors: *redefine your environment, your opportunity to create and sell a product, and your access to resources*

The **Competition** section is your opportunity to discuss your competitors.

Who, exactly, are they? Where are they? How many of them are there? Be as specific as possible in your description. The greater detail you can provide the better.

Description of Competitors Section
- Provide specific details of your competitors
- Provide key distinctions between your company and your key competitors
- Identify how you are differentiated from your key competitors
- Identify competitive advantages and disadvantages between your company and your competitors

---

Identify key distinctions between your company and your key competitors. How are you differentiated from your key competitors? Again, be as specific as possible. You should be able to identify competitive advantages and disadvantages between your company and your direct competitors.

If possible, provide a list of competitors and rank them on different attributes. Identify where are they located, what their strengths are, their weaknesses, and how you will address their strengths and weaknesses. Identify how you will compete with them on quality, pricing, promotional activities, sales activities, and any other relevant competitive aspects.

The Marketing Plan
Competition
Worksheet

Date: _____
Name: _____
Business: _____

Questions to consider:
- Who are your top three (top x) competitors?
- Who is your top (#1) competitor?
- How do they threaten you?
- What advantages do these competitors have over you?
- What advantages do you have over these competitors?
- On what basis do you compete with these competitors?
- What are you doing, or what can you do, to beat these competitors?
- Why do non-customers buy from these competitors?
- What are sales, revenue, and margin trends of you and your competitors?
- What are the benefits of your competitors' products?
- What are the key competitive issues for you against your most pressing competitors?

Reference and note all associated **Competition** expenditures on the appropriate financial spreadsheets, e.g., One-time and Start-up Costs and Expenses, Income Statement, Cash Flow Statement, Balance Sheet.

The Marketing Plan

Customers

Customers: create an opportunity for a company to create and sell a product

In the **Customer** section provide as much detail and specificity about your customers as possible. The reader expects to see that you know who your customers are, what they buy, and why. Provide information that goes beyond aggregates and group information. Be specific. Who are your customers? Where are they? What motivates them to buy from you?

In the **Marketing and Sales** sections you are talking about your customers as a defined specific segment: a Target Market. If it's possible and practical, provide individual or company names. For some commercially oriented businesses providing specific names should be quite easy.

Description of Customers Section
- Provide specific details of your customers
  - Who they are
  - What they buy
  - Wwhat they buy from you
  - Why they buy it from you
  - How they buy, e.g., bulk, impulse, re-use
  - How often do they buy
  - When, e.g., time of day, seasonally, lifecycle
  - Where do they buy

Not all prospective customers will buy your product, nor would you really want all of them to buy from you. What you are looking for are the most profitable segments of the total customer market to serve. Some are segments are easier to find; some are easier to attract; some are easier to sell, some are more willing and or able to pay, some are just plain willing to pay more. What you want to find are the segments that best suit your needs and your ability to serve. What you want to find are the segments that will provide you with the greatest profit. This is your Target Market.

Show the reader that you really know everything about your customers, your Target Market. From a banker's perspective, if you don't know who your customers are, where they are, how to reach them, and why they buy your product; why on earth would they lend you money?

If you have more than one customer segment, detail the groups and the relative information associated with each group.

One way to support an explanation of who your customers are, is to describe who you customers are not, and detail why they are not your customers.

The Marketing Plan
Customers
Worksheet

Date: _____

Name: _____

Business: _____

Questions to consider:
- Who is the primary customer target for your product/services?
- On what basis have you segmented your target customer?
- How are their needs different from other potential buyers of similar products and services?
- Why do your customers buy your product?
- What do your customers have in common?
- What are their buying patterns?
- Why do your customers buy from you and not your competitors?
- Why do others buy from your competitors and not you?
- What are customer buying patterns?
- How do you market to, and acquire customers?
- How will you market to and attract new customers to buy from your company?
- What do customers find special about your company?
- Why do you sell to the customer segments you have chosen?
- What benefits do your products provide to customers?
- How do customers learn about your product?
- How do customers acquire your products?

Reference and note all associated **Customer** expenditures on the appropriate financial spreadsheets, e.g., One-time and Start-up Costs and Expenses, Income Statement, Cash Flow Statement, Balance Sheet.

The Marketing Plan

Service / Product

The **Product/Services** section is your opportunity to list the products and services that you sell and to describe the benefits and features of your products and services.

Product / Service • List the products and services that you sell • Describe the benefits and features of your products and services

Identify what it is that you sell. What is it that your customers' value? What are the benefits of your product?

Show the reader that you have a valued product/service and get them interested in it. What's special about your product? Why do customers want it? Why do they buy it?

The Marketing Plan
Service/Product
Worksheet

Date: _____

Name: _____

Business: _____

Questions to consider:
- What are the products and services that you sell?
- Describe the features and benefits of your products and services.
- How are your products positioned, e.g., value, style, brand?
- Describe any enhanced features of your Product/Service and how they meet the needs of your target segment.
- Describe the integration of services to your product offering.
- Do you have any new product development opportunities on tap?
  - When will they be ready for market?
- Do you own any proprietary intellectual property rights?
- How are your products and services differentiated from your competitors?
- How many units do you expect to sell per quarter; per season; per year?
- Who supplies inventory, raw materials, and other product resources?

Reference and note all associated **Service/Product** expenditures on the appropriate financial spreadsheets, e.g., One-time and Start-up Costs and Expenses, Income Statement, Cash Flow Statement, Balance Sheet.

The Marketing Plan

Pricing

The **Pricing** section is your opportunity to identify your pricing strategy and to identify your prices for particular products.

Setting a price is not just arbitrarily picking a number. Price has an impact on your ability to sell, customer perception, competitive reactions, not to mention profit; so for many reasons you need to get this right.

Of the 4P's of Marketing – Product, Price, Promotion, and Place – Price is different, as it is the only one that brings in revenue. Each of the others incur expense.

> **Pricing**
> - Identify your pricing strategy
> - Identify your product pricing

Setting the right price for a product is an art. In this section discuss your pricing objectives and strategy. Discuss your prices, and how you arrived at the price chosen for your products.

Let the reader know that you have worked to maximize the price and profit opportunity available to you. Discuss the rationale you used to develop your pricing strategy and establish specific product prices.

The Marketing Plan
Pricing
Worksheet

Date: _____
Name: _____
Business: _____

Questions to consider:
- How do you price your products?
- What are the prices of your products?
- What is your pricing strategy?
- What are the goals of your pricing strategy? E.g., volume or margins?
- How does your pricing strategy align with your other marketing decisions? e.g., promotion, place, product choices.
- How does your pricing compare to your competitor's?
- Is your price consistent with the perception your customer has of your product, relative to your competitors? How so?
- Are you at the right price point(s)? How so?
- Do your prices create reasonable and acceptable margins? What are they?

Reference and note all associated **Pricing** expenditures on the appropriate financial spreadsheets, e.g., One-time and Start-up Costs and Expenses, Income Statement, Cash Flow Statement, Balance Sheet.

The Marketing Plan

Promotion/ Marketing Mix

The **Promotion** section is your opportunity to show how you will make customers aware of who you are and what you sell. Use the promotion section to identify specific promotional tools that you plan to use and their associated costs.

Promotions and advertising have three essential functions: to Inform, Persuade, and Remind. First, for your business to be successful, you must make customers aware of who you are and what you sell. You need to educate them as to the benefits of your products and you also need to persuade them why your products should be purchased over those of your competitors. Lastly you need to be consistent with a program that reminds your customers who you are, and to purchase your products.

> **Promotional Plan**
> - Inform, create awareness, and educate customers of your products/services
> - Persuade customers and prospect to buy your products your products
> - Remind customers about your company and your products

> **Promotion/Marketing Mix**
> **Promotion**
> - Sponsorship
> - Product placement
> - Endorsements
> - Merchandising
> - Public relations
> - Trade shows/events
>
> **Advertising**
> - TV
> - Radio
> - Newspapers
> - Internet
> - Mobile Phones
> - Billboard/outdoor

There are many Promotion/Advertising tools available to you. When you develop a Promotion/Advertising program, consider the total cost of each tactic as well as effectiveness, timing, reach, and of course, payback.

Not all tools are appropriate for all types of business, but virtually every business needs some promotional and advertising activities planned.

Include a Promotional Plan (see: supplemental worksheets) that outlines your promotional activities and costs for each month and explain them in detail. The totals by month can then be included in the appropriate financial statements.

The Marketing Plan
Promotion
Worksheet

Date: _____
Name: _____
Business: _____

Questions to consider:

- How will you promote your products and services?
- What do our customers read, watch, listen to, etc.?
- What is your Promotional Strategy (strategies)?
- What promotional tools do you use?
  Indirect
    o Advertising
    o Publicity
    o Sales Promotion
  Direct
    o Direct marketing
- What are your key promotional tactics?
- What are the most cost effective tools to achieve our promotional objectives?
- What are our promotional objectives?
- What control will we have over our marketing communications campaign?
- What message do we want to convey to our customers, prospects?
- What are the costs of our promotional activities?
- What sales do we expect to achieve from our promotional activities?
- What specific Promotional Tools are you planning to use?
- Why did we choose the tools we are planning to use? What are the objectives for these tools?
- What is the appropriate schedule for your promotional activities? How will these promotional programs benefit your company?
- Are they aligned properly?
- Are they cost effective?
- Are they efficient?
- Are these the best choices? Why?
- How will your Marketing efforts support your Sales efforts?

If you are planning to borrow money for marketing or promotional activities, discuss specifically how much money you need and what you are going to do with it. You will need to itemize your marketing expenses and provide detail about what you are buying. You will also need to clearly explain how those expenses are expected to result in increased revenue.

Identify specific Promotion/Marketing Mix activities. Identify costs and provide details regarding timing of activities.

If necessary, develop a supplemental financial spreadsheet and include all promotional expenses. Connect supplemental financial statements to the appropriate financial statements.

Example: Promotional Spreadsheet

Promotion/Marketing Mix

Your Business
Main St
Yourtown USA

7/1/14

Promotion	Jan	Feb	Mar	Apr	May	Jun	Jul	Aug	Sep	Oct	Nov	Dec	
sponsorship	400.00		400.00		400.00				400.00				
product placement													
endorsements													
merchandising	100.00	100.00	100.00	100.00	100.00	100.00	100.00	100.00	100.00	100.00	100.00	100.00	
public relations													
trade shows													
Advertising													
TV													
radio	600.00			600.00			600.00			600.00			
newspapers		500.00		500.00		500.00		500.00		500.00		500.00	
Internet	300.00	300.00	300.00	300.00	300.00	300.00		300.00	300.00	300.00	300.00	300.00	
Mobile Phones													
													Total
	1,400.00	900.00	800.00	1,500.00	800.00	900.00	700.00	900.00	800.00	1,500.00	400.00	900.00	11,500.00

Notes and assumptions:

THE BUSINESS PLAN WORKBOOK

© E Clark 2014

Reference and note all associated **Promotion** expenditures on the appropriate financial spreadsheets, e.g., One-time and Start-up Costs and Expenses, Income Statement, Cash Flow Statement, Balance Sheet.

THE
BUSINESS PLAN
WORKBOOK

The Marketing Plan

Distribution/Location and Facilities (Place)

The **Distribution/Location and Facilities (Place)** section is your opportunity to show how you will put your products in the hands of your customers. The purpose of the Distribution/Location and Facilities (Place) section is to identify your distribution strategy; your channels of distribution and to discuss channel functions and responsibilities as well as your location and facilities.

Include as part of the **Distribution (Place) discussion** your choices as they relate to Coverage, Channel choices, and allocation of Channel Functions.

Description of Distribution/Location and Facilities
- Identify your distribution strategy
- Identify your channels of distribution
- Discuss channel functions and responsibilities
- Discuss your location
- Discuss your facilities

Discuss relevant issues as they relate to your the **Location and Facilities.**

Of the 4P's of Marketing, (Product, Price, Promotion, and Place), Place is perhaps the most difficult to control or to make adjustments.

Choices and control of distribution, in particular, can often be extremely limited. Access to distribution channels, or lack of, can make or break a business. For many small businesses, location is often their only source of competitive advantage.

The Marketing Plan
Distribution/Location and Facilities (Place)
Worksheet

Date: _____
Name: _____
Business: _____

Distribution - Questions to consider:
- What market coverage strategy is most appropriate? Why?
  - Intensive distribution
  - Selective distribution
  - Exclusive distribution
- How will you get your product/service to your customers?
  - Where do they want it?
  - When they want it?
  - How do they want it?
- What channels will you sell through?
- What coverage strategy best suits your market and product choices?
- What channels will best distribute your product? What best suits your customers? Your product?
- Who will perform what channel functions? The channels? You?
- What key channel functions will you assume? Your channels?
  e.g., Transactional, logistical, facilitating
  - How will this affect your business?
- What combination of coverage, channels, and function responsibilities will be most profitable?

Location and Facilities - Questions to consider:
- What are the key attributes of your location & facilities?
  - Access?
  - Parking?
  - Layout?
  - Square footage?
  - Lighting?
  - Furniture?
- How will your location impact sales?
- How will your facility impact sales?
- What are the costs associated with your location and facilities?
- What are the customer benefits from your location and facilities?

Identify **Distribution** costs on the appropriate worksheets:
> **Start-up and One-time Expenses** (expenses)
> **Capital Equipment** (costs)
> **Operating Expenses** (expenses)

Identify and list associated **Distribution** costs in the appendix with supplier sources and associated costs.

Reference and note all associated
Distribution/Location and Facilities (Place)
expenditures on the appropriate financial
spreadsheets, e.g., One-time and Start-up Costs and
Expenses, Income Statement, Cash Flow Statement,
Balance Sheet.

THE
BUSINESS PLAN
WORKBOOK

The Business Plan Workbook

The Sales Plan

The **Sales Plan** section is your opportunity to define your sales goals and objectives and to describe how you plan to create sales.

> **The Sales Plan**
> The Sales Team
> Sales Management
> Sales Policies
> Sales Projections

There are four main topics that should be covered as part of the Sales Plan; the Sales Team, Sales Management, Sales Policies, and your Sales Projections.

The **Sales Team** includes all those involved with selling your product including direct and in-direct channels and sales partners.

The **Sales Management** section should identify who will be responsible for leading the sales team and responsible for achieving sales goals.

> **The Sales Plan**
> • Identify your sales goals and objectives
> • Describe your sales process to achieve your sales goals and objectives
> • Identify how you plan to achieve your sales goals
> • Describe the management of your sales team

The **Sales Policies** section is used to discuss sales policies and the sales tools that the company plans on using to achieve sales goals.

Sales Projections are estimates of future sales over a specified period of time. Sales projections should be broken out by meaningful categories, such as by product, product type or category, sales by region, by sales person, location, etc, over a specified period of time. **Sales Projections** are a key component of the business plan and in all likelihood they will be scrutinized.

- **How much money is being requested?** Are you looking to fund sales operations for the business? If so, how much money do you need? Be specific, e.g., X amount for expenses, Y amount for equipment.
- **What are you going to do with the money?** Itemize amounts. Again, be specific, e.g., provide a list of expenses; a list of the equipment. A key question the reader wants to know here is whether the requested funds will produce new revenues and new profits.
- **How long do you need it for?** Weeks, months, years?
- **How the funds will be repaid?** Will requested funds be paid from new revenues or existing cash flows? Will new equipment create new products and cash flow?
- **How can you assure me that I will get my money back?** If you are acquiring new assets can they be in part used as collateral? What else can you offer as an assurance of repayment?

The Sales Plan
Introduction
Worksheet

Date: _____

Name: _____

Business: _____

The Sales Team - Questions to consider:
- Do you have an inside or outside direct sales force?
- Do you have sales/channel partners?
- How are they arranged? e.g., geographically, by industry, product
- How will they be monitored?

Sales Management - Questions to consider:
- What is the structure of your sales management team?
- What are the sales goals for the management team?

Sales Policies - Questions to consider:
- What are your sales quotas by product line, sales person, region or whatever metric is appropriate?
- What latitude do your sales channels have to adjust prices?
- How will returns affect sales goals and commissions?
- How will channels be compensated?
- What sales promotions will you use? When?
- What will sales promotions cost you in dollars and lost revenue?

Sales Projections - Questions to consider:
- How much will you sell?
- When will you sell it?
- What is the total Market Sales Opportunity available?
- What is your business' maximum available capacity? Quantity? Percentage?
- If you are adding new equipment, personnel, etc., how does this impact your maximum capacity? Quantity? Percentage?
- What strategy and tactics do you plan to implement to increase sales?
- What is the average industry price for your product?
  o How does your price compare?
- What are your estimated costs per unit?
  o Fixed costs, Variable costs e.g., raw materials, labor, utilities, etc.

Develop and provide Supplemental Financial spreadsheets for sales projections and include COGS.

THE BUSINESS PLAN WORKBOOK

The Sales Plan

The Sales Team

The **Sales Team** involves all those involved with selling your product including direct and in-direct channels and sales partners. Identify how many sales people you have, who they are, their roles and responsibilities, and indicate their individual sales goals.

Typically, when you involve sales channels or partners there is a trade-off between costs and control. While sales channels can be a cost effective route to increase sales or reduce expenses, they are often more difficult to manage and control.

The Sales Team
- Identify the structure of your sales team and the overall sales goals
- Identify your sales team and their individual goals, including direct and indirect sales channels
- Discuss how you will manage the sales team, channels

When developing sales channels, consider your objectives, degree of control, and cost effectiveness. You want to create a program that aligns your tactics and meets your objectives as cost effectively as possible.

The Sales Team
Direct Sales
- Outside sales
- Inside sales
- Service
Indirect Sales
- Sales Partners
- Channels

Identify your sales channel partners and sales employees. Discuss why you have chosen the channels you have and how you will manage them. Provide background on individuals if relevant.

Identify who they are and what their sales goals are. Describe the process each sales team group will be using. For example, if you will have an in-house sales group or an external sales group and any sales channels you plan to use. Identify how each group will be measured, compensated and how you will manage their performance.

The Sales Plan
The Sales Team
Worksheet

Date: _____

Name: _____

Business: _____

Questions to consider:
- Do you have an inside or outside direct sales force?
- Do you have sales/channel partners?
- What are the sales goals for your sales team?
- Who comprises your sales team?
- How many members of the team are there?
- How is the sales team arranged? e.g., geographically, by industry, product
- How will they be monitored?
- How will they be measured?
- How will they be compensated?
- Discuss your direct sales force.
  - What is the structure of your sales team?
  - How many sales people?
  - Where are they?
  - What do they sell?
  - How will they be compensated?
- Discuss your in-direct sales force.
  - What is the structure of this team?
  - What is the contractual relationship with your in-direct sales force?
  - How many sales people?
  - Where are they?
  - What do they sell?
  - How will they be compensated?

Reference and note all associated **Sales Team** expenditures on the appropriate financial spreadsheets, e.g., One-time and Start-up Costs and Expenses, Income Statement, Cash Flow Statement, Balance Sheet.

The Sales Plan

Sales Management

The **Sales Management** section should identify who will be responsible for achieving sale goals and managing the Sales Team.

Use this section to identify the sales management team and how the sales team will be managed. Discuss the roles and responsibilities of the Sales Management team and how the sales force will be structured.

Also include in this section how the sales management will develop and manage sales channels.

Provide the background on individuals if it is relevant and will advance your business plan.

Highlight the structure of the Sales Team, the Sales Management team, key Sales Policies, and mention aggregate sales forecast estimates.

Sales Management
- Identify the sales management team
- Discuss the management of the sales team
- Discuss the development and management of sales policies and procedures
- Discuss the development and management of sales channels

The Sales Plan
Sales Management
Worksheet

Date: _____

Name: _____

Business: _____

Questions to consider:

- What is the structure of your sales management team?
  - How many sales people do they manage?
  - Where are they?
- What are the sales goals for the management team?
- How will they be monitored?
- How will they be measured?
- How will they be compensated?
- Include an organizational chart of the sales team.

Reference and note all associated **Sales Management** expenditures on the appropriate financial spreadsheets, e.g., One-time and Start-up Costs and Expenses, Income Statement, Cash Flow Statement, Balance Sheet.

The Sales Plan

Sales Policies

Identify **Sales Policies** and discuss how the company plans on using these policies to achieve its sales goals.

Some basic Sales Policies for consideration include:
- Sales quotas
- Pricing latitude for sales reps and channels
- Return policies
- Commissions
- Sales promotions
- Up-selling, cross-selling

Identify the latitude sales people have to utilize discretionary sales policies such as returns and discounts.

Sales Policies
- Identify your sales policies and tools
- Discuss the use of sales tools by the sales force and sales channels

---

The Sales Plan
Sales Policies
Worksheet

Date: _____

Name: _____

Business: _____

Questions to consider:

Quotas:
- What is the appropriate metric to measure sales quotas?
- What are your sales quotas by product line, sales person, region, or whatever metric is appropriate?

Pricing latitude:
- Do your sales people have any opportunity to adjust prices?
- What latitude do your sales channels have to adjust prices?
- Do your sales people and sales channels compete with each other for sales?
  - o Is this a problem?

Returns policies:
- What is your return policy?
- How will returns affect sales goals and commissions?

Commissions:
- What is your commission structure? When will sales people be paid?
- How will channels be compensated?

Sales promotions:
- What sales promotions will you use? When?
- What will sales promotions cost you in dollars and lost revenue?
- What return do you hope to achieve in revenue from sales promotions?

Up-selling, cross-selling:
- What up-selling or cross-selling opportunities do you have?
- Up-selling, cross-selling sales quotas?

Reference and note all associated **Sales Policies** expenditures on the appropriate financial spreadsheets, e.g., One-time and Start-up Costs and Expenses, Income Statement, Cash Flow Statement, Balance Sheet.

The Sales Plan

Sales Projections

The importance of the sales forecast cannot be overstated. When creating a pro forma financial statement, the sales forecast will perhaps be the most important estimate that you make. **Sales Projections** are a key component of the business plan and in all likelihood they will be scrutinized. Special care must be given to provide clear and unambiguous explanations of all projections.

> **Sales Forecast/Estimate**
> - Provide an estimate of future levels of sales and revenue at a given price
> - Provide an estimate of COGS (cost of goods sold)

Your **Sales Forecast should** provide an estimate of future levels of sales and revenue over time, at a given price. Include as part of your sales projections an estimate of COGS (cost of goods sold).

The two key questions a sales estimate should answer are:
At a given price:
- How much will you sell?
- When will you sell it?

Sales estimates (projections) impact every aspect of a business including: sales and marketing efforts and expenditures, capital equipment investments, production schedules, operational cash-flow, the acquisition of inventory, procurement schedules for raw materials, and staffing and personnel needs for the business.

Develop supplemental financial spreadsheets for your sales projections and include COGS. Connect supplemental financial statements to the appropriate financial statements.

Typically, sales forecasts provide a per unit quantity at a specific price, over a certain time frame. Sales estimates should be broken out by meaningful categories such as by product, product type or category, sales by region, by sales person, location, etc. The finer the degree of clarity or granularity in a sales forecast, the better.

> **Sales Projection (Revenue)**
> Unit (volume) x selling price = revenue

The timeframe is usually one year by month, but depending on the business or the need they may be quarterly or even weekly.

The Sales Plan
Sales Projections
Worksheet

Date: _____

Name: _____

Business: _____

Questions to consider:

- What do your sales estimates reflect, e.g., a new business, a new product line, new equipment, new marketing or sales efforts?

- What are you selling? Describe your products:
  Mfg: product(s)
  Service: labor/service
  Reseller   product(s)

- What is the maximum estimated capacity of your business (new product line, new equipment, new marketing or sales efforts)?
- What is your sale unit? (e.g., per product, per sales rep, per day, per piece of equipment)
- How many units will you sell daily, weekly, monthly, annually?
- What is the per unit selling price?
- What is the total available market sales opportunity?
- What percentage of the total available market sales opportunity are you attempting to capture?
- At your estimated sales level, at what percentage of capacity will your business be operating?
  - How does your sales levels and capacity utilization compare to others in your industry?
- If you are adding new equipment, personnel, etc., how does this impact your current operations?
- If you are adding new equipment, personnel, etc., how much of an increase is it to your current maximum capacity? Quantity? Percentage?
- Do you have access to historical industry sales data? If yes,
  - Where did you get it?
  - How does it compare to your sales estimates?
- Do you have actual historical company sales data? If yes,
  - Where did you get it?
  - How does it compare to your estimates?

- What industry data do you have available to support your sales estimates?
- What is the average industry price for your product?
    o How does your price compare?
    o How will your price impact your sales levels?

COGS (Cost of Goods Sold) Estimates
- How are industry COGS affected by seasonality?
- What industry data do you have available to support your COGS estimates?
- What are your estimated costs per unit?
    o Fixed costs, variable costs e.g., raw materials

Develop and provide supplemental financial spreadsheets for sales projections and include COGS.

Note: Provide detailed explanations and assumptions for your sales estimates.

Example: Sales Estimate - 1 Year w/COGS

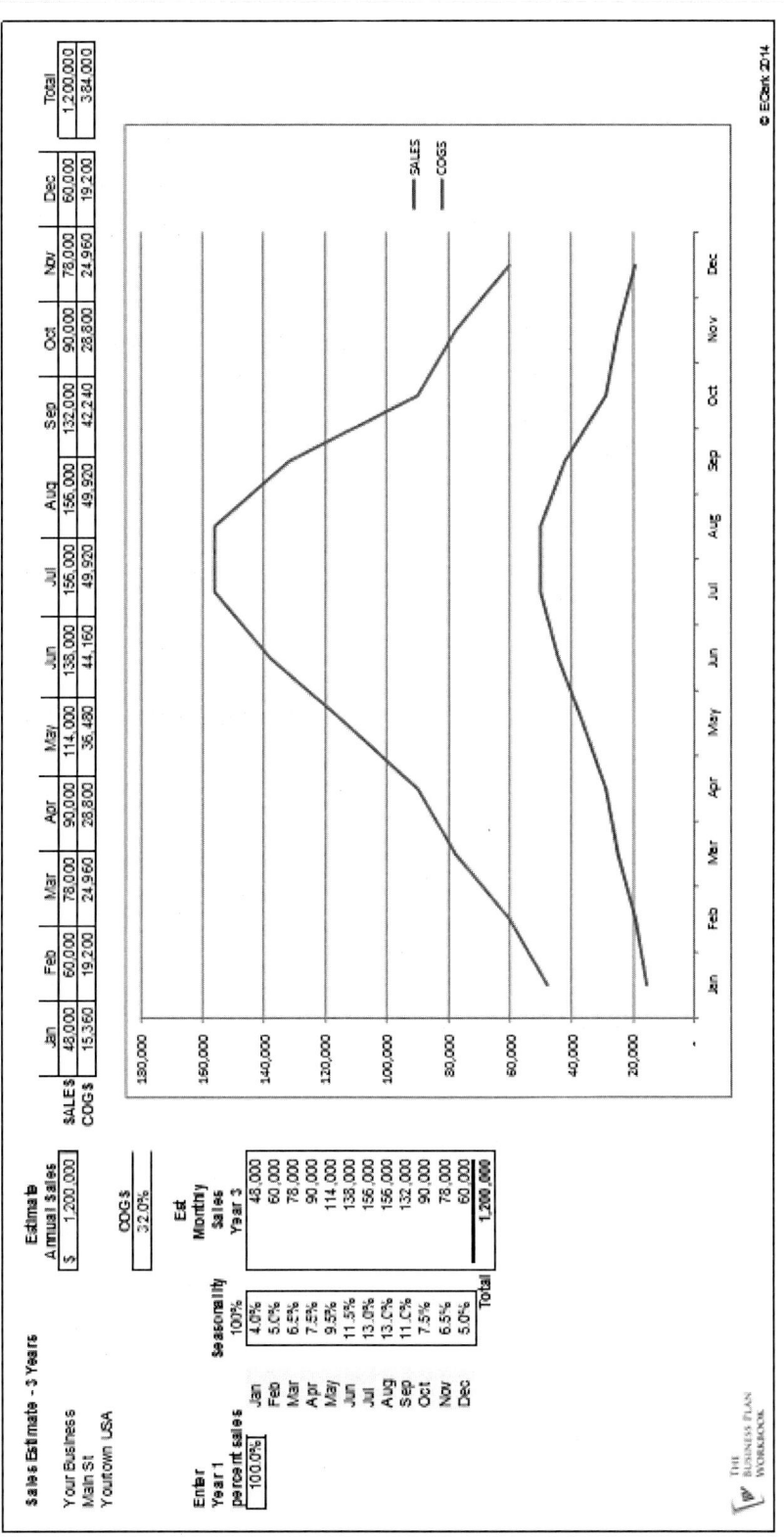

This example provides a total sales estimate with an estimate percentage COGS.

This example was developed using a top-down approach, estimating total sales and then allocating sales monthly based on estimated percentage seasonality.

The example on the next page follows the same approach and provides estimated sales and COGS for three years.

The Business Plan Workbook

Example: Sales Estimate - 3 Years

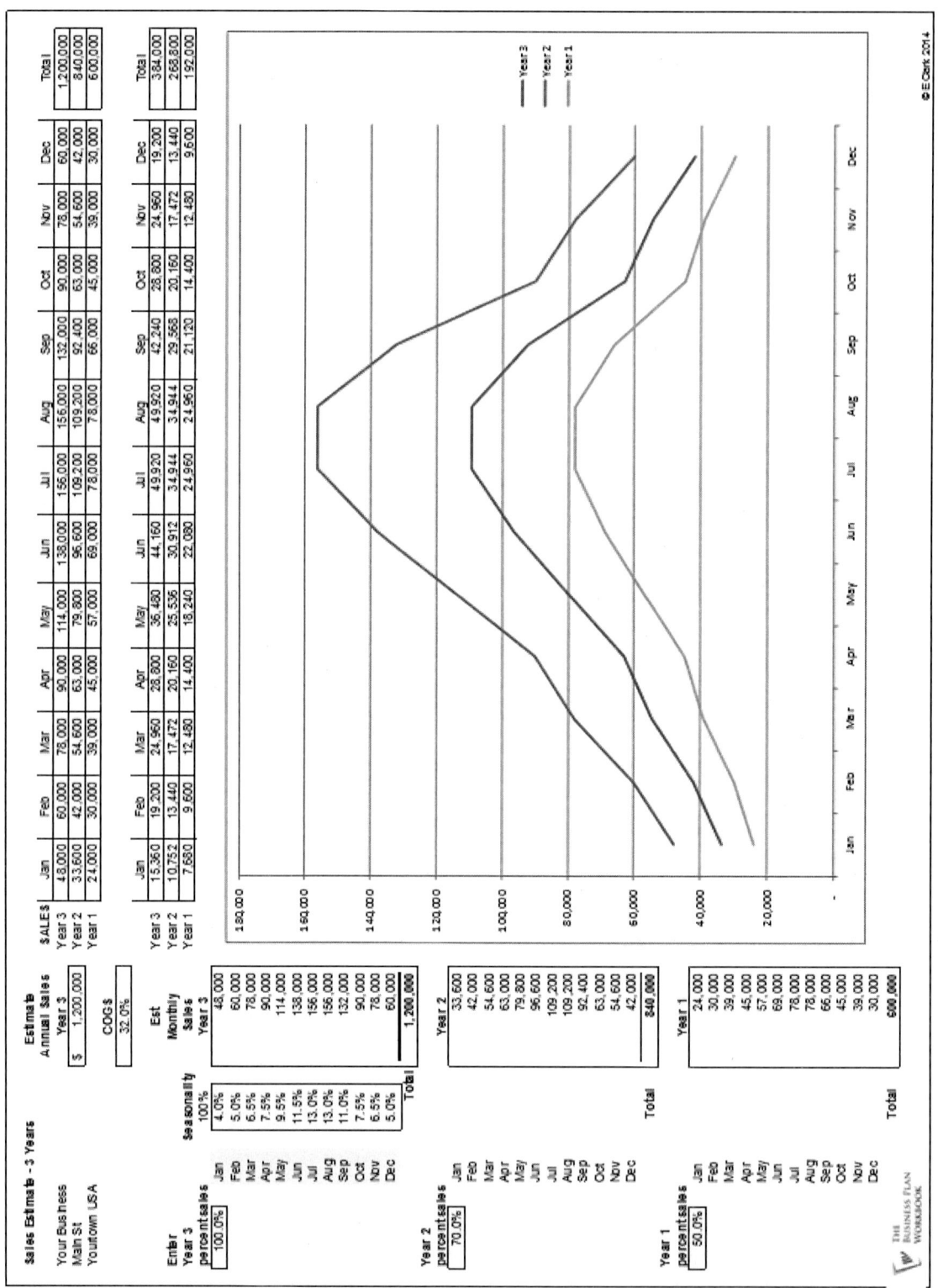

Sales Estimate - 3 Years

Your Business
Main St
Yourtown USA

Estimate Annual Sales	
Year 3	$ 1,200,000
COG$	32.0%

SALES	Jan	Feb	Mar	Apr	May	Jun	Jul	Aug	Sep	Oct	Nov	Dec	Total
Year 3	48,000	60,000	78,000	90,000	114,000	138,000	156,000	156,000	132,000	90,000	78,000	60,000	1,200,000
Year 2	33,600	42,000	54,600	63,000	79,800	96,600	109,200	109,200	92,400	63,000	54,600	42,000	840,000
Year 1	24,000	30,000	39,000	45,000	57,000	69,000	78,000	78,000	66,000	45,000	39,000	30,000	600,000

COG$	Jan	Feb	Mar	Apr	May	Jun	Jul	Aug	Sep	Oct	Nov	Dec	Total
Year 3	15,360	19,200	24,960	28,800	36,480	44,160	49,920	49,920	42,240	28,800	24,960	19,200	384,000
Year 2	10,752	13,440	17,472	20,160	25,536	30,912	34,944	34,944	29,568	20,160	17,472	13,440	268,800
Year 1	7,680	9,600	12,480	14,400	18,240	22,080	24,960	24,960	21,120	14,400	12,480	9,600	192,000

Enter Year 3

	percent sales / Seasonality 100%	Est Monthly Sales Year 3
	100.0%	
Jan	4.0%	48,000
Feb	5.0%	60,000
Mar	6.5%	78,000
Apr	7.5%	90,000
May	9.5%	114,000
Jun	11.5%	138,000
Jul	13.0%	156,000
Aug	13.0%	156,000
Sep	11.0%	132,000
Oct	7.5%	90,000
Nov	6.5%	78,000
Dec	5.0%	60,000
Total		1,200,000

Year 2 percent sales	70.0%
Jan	33,600
Feb	42,000
Mar	54,600
Apr	63,000
May	79,800
Jun	96,600
Jul	109,200
Aug	109,200
Sep	92,400
Oct	63,000
Nov	54,600
Dec	42,000
Total	840,000

Year 1 percent sales	50.0%
Jan	24,000
Feb	30,000
Mar	39,000
Apr	45,000
May	57,000
Jun	69,000
Jul	78,000
Aug	78,000
Sep	66,000
Oct	45,000
Nov	39,000
Dec	30,000
Total	600,000

Legend: Year 3, Year 2, Year 1

THE BUSINESS PLAN WORKBOOK

Example: Sales Estimate – 1 Year

Sales Estimates by Product

Your Business
Main St
Yourtown USA

	January	February	March	April	May	June	July	August	September	October	November	December		Totals
1 Windshield Replacements	28,800	36,000	46,800	54,000	68,400	82,800	93,600	93,600	79,200	54,000	46,800	36,000		720,000
2 Repalcements (Wholesale Clients)	12,000	15,000	19,500	22,500	28,500	34,500	39,000	39,000	33,000	22,500	19,500	15,000		300,000
3 Repairs	7,200	9,000	11,700	13,500	17,100	20,700	23,400	23,400	19,800	13,500	11,700	9,000		180,000
4	-	-	-	-	-	-	-	-	-	-	-	-		-
5														-
6														-
7														-
Total Sales	$ 48,000	$ 60,000	$ 78,000	$ 90,000	$ 114,000	$ 138,000	$ 156,000	$ 156,000	$ 132,000	$ 90,000	$ 78,000	$ 60,000		$ 1,200,000
est TTL COGS	$ 14,400	$ 18,000	$ 23,400	$ 27,000	$ 34,200	$ 41,400	$ 46,800	$ 46,800	$ 39,600	$ 27,000	$ 23,400	$ 18,000		$ 360,000	30%
est Gross margin	$ 33,600	$ 42,000	$ 54,600	$ 63,000	$ 79,800	$ 96,600	$ 109,200	$ 109,200	$ 92,400	$ 63,000	$ 54,600	$ 42,000		$ 840,000	70%

Product 1
Windshield Replacements

			average Unit selling price	est cost	Notes:	
Mfg:	product(s)				**Installations for truck 1**	
Service:	labor/service	installation	200			
Reseller	product(s)	Windshields	200	120	labor cost included in wages - consider fixed	
			400	120		

	January	February	March	April	May	June	July	August	September	October	November	December	
Units sales	72	90	117	135	171	207	234	234	198	135	117	90	
price	400	400	400	400	400	400	400	400	400	400	400	400	
est rev	$ 28,800	$ 36,000	$ 46,800	$ 54,000	$ 68,400	$ 82,800	$ 93,600	$ 93,600	$ 79,200	$ 54,000	$ 46,800	$ 36,000	$ 720,000.00
est COGS	8,640	10,800	14,040	16,200	20,520	24,840	28,080	28,080	23,760	16,200	14,040	10,800	$ 216,000.00	30%
prod gross margin	20,160	25,200	32,760	37,800	47,880	57,960	65,520	65,520	55,440	37,800	32,760	25,200	$ 504,000.00	70%

This example provides a sales estimate summary for a business with 3 product lines.

The example provides the summary of three products lines and details for one of the product lines.

> Reference and note all associated **Sales Estimates** to the appropriate financial spreadsheets, e.g., One-time and Start-up Costs and Expenses, Income Statement, Cash Flow Statement, Balance Sheet.

THE
BUSINESS PLAN
WORKBOOK

Financial Documentation

Financial Documentation is the second major section of the Business Plan. This section provides the financial details and accounting of your operations as to where the money came in and where the money went out.

The financial section documents revenues and expenses and accounts for financial performance through standardized financial statements and supplemental supporting documents.

Financial Statements are standard accounting documents that are used to report financial transactions and account for business operations. There are four standard financial statements.

Financial Statements
Income Statement
Cash Flow Statement
Balance Sheet
Statement of Shareholders' Equity

Supplemental Financial Statements (or Documents) add detail and explanations to the Financial Statements to make the standardized documents cleaner and easier to read and understand.

Supplemental Financial Documents
Sources and Uses of Funds Statement
Capital Equipment
Start Up Costs (One-Time Expenses)
Loan Application
Sales Estimates
Wages/Salaries
Marketing – Promotional Expenses
Loan Repayments Schedule
Depreciation Schedule

Financial Statements

Financial Statements are standard accounting documents that are used to report financial transactions and account for business operations. There are four standard financial statements.

Income Statement

The **Income Statement** (Profit & Loss Statement or P&L) accounts for income and expenses for the business during the accounting period. The Income Statement indicates if the company has been profitable.

Cash Flow Statement

The **Cash Flow Statement** reports actual receipts and disbursements of cash for the business during the accounting period. The Cash Flow Statement indicates if the company has the necessary cash available to pay debts.

Balance Sheet

The **Balance Sheet** is used to indicate the assets, liabilities, and shareholders' equity in the business at a given point in time. The Balance Sheet shows what a company owns and what it owes.

Statement of Shareholders' Equity

The **Statement of Shareholders' Equity** shows the changes of value of the owners' equity over an accounting period. The Statement of Shareholders' Equity indicates any owner investments, dividends paid, or operational gain or loss. Essentially, the Statement of Shareholders' Equity indicates the impact of business operations on owners' wealth during the accounting period .

Two general points about developing and presenting Financial Statements;

    1. Use standard formats
    2. Explain and document the numbers

1. Use standard formats

Use a standard format for your financial statements. A standard format will make them easy to read. If the bank has a preference for particular format, use theirs. *This is not the place to be creative.*

Fit each financial statement to one page. For example, the Income Statement and the Cash Flow Analysis should each be on a single page.

While you want each Financial Statement to fit on one page, it is also extremely important that numbers can be read. Spend the time necessary to make the numbers readable.

2. Explain and document the numbers

Numbers require an explanation; particularly for Pro forma financial statements. Pro forma financial statements without adequate explanations and documentation are by themselves of little value.

Pro forma numbers are expectations based on assumptions. The reader wants to know those assumptions and "where the numbers come from." The numbers alone are not self-evident.

Provide extensive footnoting and explanations. Documentation will make the Financial Statements easier to read. Strive to create intuitive Supplemental Financial Documents that the banker can easily associate with the Financial Statements.

Make the financial statements easy to understand by documenting them, explaining them, and using a consistent format. Relate the numbers to the text from your plan. Make certain that the reader can identify where the numbers on the Income Statement, the Balance Sheet, etc., originate from within the text.

Income Statement

The **Income Statement** (Profit and Loss Statement or P&L) accounts for income and expenses for the business during the accounting period. The Income Statement indicates if the company has been profitable.

The purpose of the Income Statement is to show managers and investors whether or not the company made or lost money during the period being reported.

The **Income Statement** presents the financial results of the business' revenue and expenses over a particular period of time.

Income Statement
- Report the income the business earned during the accounting period
- Report the expenses that were incurred during that period
- Report the difference between the incomes and expenses for that period, as net profit (or loss)

The Income Statement shows how Net Revenue (money received from the sale of products and services before expenses, aka, the "top line") was transformed into Net Income (the result after all revenues and expenses have been accounted for, aka, the "bottom line").

The Income Statement has five basic sections.
Sections of the Income Statement:
- Net Sales
- Cost of Goods Sold
- Gross Margin
- Expenses
- Net Income (or loss)

Net Sales minus Cost of Goods Sold equals Gross Margin. Gross Margin minus Expenses equals Net Income (or loss)

Net Sales and Cost of Goods Sold are found on the Sales Estimates/Sales Forecast.

COGS is a variable expense. The more units you sell, the greater the COGS. Generally, Expenses are fixed costs. For example, rent is $X per month whether you sell one unit or 50.

Accounting Equation: Income Statement
Profit = Revenue – Expenses

The Income Statement Worksheet

Date: _____

Name: _____

Business: _____

This is an example of an Income Statement for a small business

Income Statement	Year 3													7/11/14
Your Business Main St Yourtown USA														
	MONTH													
	Jan	Feb	Mar	Apr	May	Jun	Jul	Aug	Sep	Oct	Nov	Dec	TOTAL	%
Total Sales	48,000	60,000	78,000	90,000	114,000	138,000	156,000	156,000	132,000	90,000	78,000	60,000	1,200,000	100%
Cost of Goods Sold	15,360	19,200	24,960	28,800	36,480	44,160	49,920	49,920	42,240	28,800	24,960	19,200	384,000	32%
Gross Profit	32,640	40,800	53,040	61,200	77,520	93,840	106,080	106,080	89,760	61,200	53,040	40,800	816,000	68.0%
Operating Expenses														
1 Wages - Salaries	17,400	17,400	17,400	27,792	27,792	27,792	27,792	27,792	20,880	20,880	20,880	20,880	274,680	22.9%
2 Rent	7,000	7,000	7,000	7,000	7,000	7,000	7,000	7,000	7,000	7,000	7,000	7,000	84,000	7.0%
3 Utilities, elec	5,000	5,000	5,000	5,000	5,000	5,000	5,000	5,000	5,000	5,000	5,000	5,000	60,000	5.0%
4 Sales, General and Admin	6,000	6,000	6,000	6,000	6,000	6,000	6,000	6,000	6,000	6,000	6,000	6,000	72,000	6.0%
5 Accounting / Legal	800	800	800	800	800	800	800	800	800	800	800	800	9,600	0.8%
6 Mktg - Promotion	1,400	900	800	1,500	800	900	1,000	900	800	1,500	400	900	11,800	1.0%
7 Insurance	1,400	1,400	1,400	1,400	1,400	1,400	1,400	1,400	1,400	1,400	1,400	1,400	16,800	1.4%
8 Auto Expenses	2,000	2,000	2,000	2,000	2,000	2,000	2,000	2,000	2,000	2,000	2,000	2,000	24,000	2.0%
9 L-T Loan	2,090	2,090	2,090	2,090	2,090	2,090	2,090	2,090	2,090	2,090	2,090	2,090	25,081	2.1%
10 S-T Loan	4,328	2,297	1,060										7,685	0.6%
11 Operating Supplies	800	800	800	800	800	800	800	800	800	800	800	800	9,600	0.8%
12 Repairs/ Maintenance	1,000	1,000	1,000	1,000	1,000	1,000	1,000	1,000	1,000	1,000	1,000	1,000	12,000	1.0%
13 Depreciation	4,800	4,800	4,800	4,800	4,800	4,800	4,800	4,800	4,800	4,800	4,800	4,800	57,600	4.8%
14														
15														
16														
17														
18														
19														
20														
Total Expenses	54,018	51,487	50,150	60,182	59,482	59,582	59,682	59,582	52,570	53,270	52,170	52,670	664,846	55.4%
Net Profit Before Tax	(21,378)	(10,687)	2,890	1,018	18,038	34,258	46,398	46,498	37,190	7,930	870	(11,870)	151,154	12.6%

Notes:

© E Clark 2014

THE BUSINESS PLAN WORKBOOK

Cash Flow Statement

The Cash Flow Statement presents cash receipts and cash disbursements over a particular period of time. The purpose of the **Cash Flow Statement** is to show whether or not the company increased or decreased its available cash position during the period reported.

The Cash Flow Statement shows how much cash is available on hand, and if the company has the ability to pay its current debts.

In many ways, the Cash Flow Statement and the Income Statement appear to be fairly similar. They look fairly similar and have much of the same detail. The difference between the two is that the Cash Flow Statement reports cash transactions, not income. Cash and Income are not equivalent. The Cash Flow Statement provides insight to the financial health of a company.

> **Cash Flow Statement**
> - Report the cash inflows to the business during the accounting period
> - Report the cash outflows from the business during the accounting period
> - Report the net change in cash during the accounting period

Depending upon the timing of cash receipts, a business can be profitable from the perspective of the Income Statement, yet unable to pay its bills. The Income Statement shows Income, not Cash. When a sale is made it is booked as income even if the business has not yet been paid. The Cash Flow Statement shows cash, not income. The Cash Flow Statement records the receipts only when cash is received (or disbursed).

For many businesses, there is a time lag between when a sale is made and when payment is received. Therefore you can be "profitable," yet have no money, and therefore unable to pay your bills.

On the next page there is an example of a Cash flow Statement that shows startup costs, and negative cash flow for the first four months with short term borrowing (line-of-credit) for the first three and an equity investment in month four of operations of a business.

Accounting Equation: Cash Flow
Cash Flow = Receipts – Disbursements

The Cash flow Statement Worksheet

Date: _____

Name: _____

Business: _____

Cash Flow — Year 1 — 7/1/14

Your Business
Main St
Yourtown USA

#	Account	Start Up	Jan	Feb	Mar	Apr	May	Jun	Jul	Aug	Sep	Oct	Nov	Dec	TOTAL	%
	Income from Sales															
	Cash Receipts/Sales		24,000	30,000	39,000	45,000	57,000	69,000	78,000	78,000	66,000	45,000	39,000	30,000	600,000	100%
	Disbursements															
1	Inventory (COGS)		7,680	9,600	12,480	14,400	18,240	22,080	24,960	24,960	21,120	14,400	12,480	9,600	192,000	32%
2	Wages - Salaries		10,440	10,440	10,440	13,920	13,920	13,920	13,920	13,920	13,920	13,920	13,920	13,920	156,600	26%
3	Rent		2,800	2,800	2,800	2,800	2,800	2,800	2,800	2,800	2,800	2,800	2,800	2,800	33,600	6%
4	Utilities, elec		3,400	3,400	3,400	3,400	3,400	3,400	3,400	3,400	3,400	3,400	3,400	3,400	40,800	7%
5	Sales, General and Admin		2,600	2,600	2,600	2,600	2,600	2,600	2,600	2,600	2,600	2,600	2,600	2,600	31,200	5%
6	Mktg - Promotion		800	800	800	800	800	800	800	800	800	800	800	800	9,600	2%
7	Insurance		1,400	900	800	1,500	800	900	700	900	800	1,500	400	900	11,500	2%
8	Auto Expenses		1,500	1,500	1,500	1,500	1,500	1,500	1,500	1,500	1,500	1,500	1,500	1,500	18,000	3%
9	L-T Loan		1,800	1,800	1,800	1,800	1,800	1,800	1,800	1,800	1,800	1,800	1,800	1,800	21,600	4%
10	S-T Loan		2,090	2,090	2,090	2,090	2,090	2,090	2,090	2,090	2,090	2,090	2,090	2,090	25,081	4%
11	Operating Supplies		-	2,756	3,586	3,940	3,940	3,940	3,940	3,940	3,940	3,940	3,940	3,940	41,799	7%
12	Repairs/ Maintenance		340	340	340	340	340	340	340	340	340	340	340	340	4,080	1%
13	Depreciation		350	350	350	350	350	350	350	350	350	350	350	350	4,200	1%
14																
15																
16																
17																
18																
19																
20															-	0%
	Total Disbursed		35,200	39,376	42,986	49,440	52,580	56,520	59,200	59,400	55,460	49,440	46,420	44,040	590,060	98%

Account	Start Up	Jan	Feb	Mar	Apr	May	Jun	Jul	Aug	Sep	Oct	Nov	Dec	TOTAL
Cash flow from Operations		(11,200)	(9,376)	(3,986)	(4,440)	4,420	12,480	18,800	18,600	10,540	(4,440)	(7,420)	(14,040)	Year 1
L-T Loan Receipts	200,000													-
S-T Loan Receipts	20,000	11,200	9,400	4,000										24,600 *(Line of Credit)*
Equity Invested	83,550				4,500									4,500
Cash flow from Financing	303,550	11,200	9,400	4,000	4,500									Year 1

Start up Expenses:

	Start Up
Capital Equipment List	250,000
One Time Start up Costs	14,900
Misc Equipment	3,100
Supplies and Expenses	15,550
Inventory	20,000
Total Start up Expenses	303,550

Account	Start Up	Jan	Feb	Mar	Apr	May	Jun	Jul	Aug	Sep	Oct	Nov	Dec
NET Cash flow	-	(0)	24	14	60	4,420	12,480	18,800	18,600	10,540	(4,440)	(7,420)	(14,040)
Beginning Cash Balance	-	-	(0)	24	37	98	4,518	16,998	35,798	54,399	64,939	60,499	53,079
Ending Cash Balance	-	(0)	24	37	98	4,518	16,998	35,798	54,399	64,939	60,499	53,079	39,040

Notes:

THE BUSINESS PLAN WORKBOOK

The Business Plan Workbook

Balance Sheet

The Balance Sheet is a statement that shows the company's financial position *at a given point in time*. The Balance Sheet is used to show the book value of assets, liabilities, and shareholders' equity in the business. The Balance Sheet shows what a company owns and what it owes.

The Balance Sheet is often referred to as a "snapshot", as it shows a picture of the business at a specific point in time. A Balance sheet does not provide any relative information regarding the flow of volume, rate of changes, or velocity of the business. It merely states where the business stands, without providing insight as to how the business arrived here, or where it's going.

> **Balance Sheet**
> - Report the company's financial position at a particular point in time
> - Report the value of assets, liabilities and owners' equity in the business

When you have more than one year of Balance Sheets available, you can determine a degree of financial change the business has achieved.

One use of the Balance Sheet is to provide a creditor with information regarding potential assets that might be pledged as collateral. A strong Balance Sheet shows a potential creditor that if all else fails, that they can get their money back from the sale of assets.

On the next page there is an example of a Pro forma Balance Sheet. This Balance Sheet is unusual as it has two additional columns to help in the development of a Pro forma Balance Sheet. The first column shows the balance for a business, with an all cash position, End of Day 0. The second column shows the balance as if all the cash had been spent to start the business all in day, End of Day 1. This "trick" helps to establish an opening Balance for the business and a reference point when developing a Pro forma Balance Sheet.

> **Accounting Equation: Balance Sheet**
> Assets = Owners Equity + Liabilities
> Liabilities = Assets − Owner's Equity
> Owner's Equity = Assets − Liabilities

The Balance Sheet
Worksheet

Date: _____

Name: _____

Business: _____

Balance Sheet	Year 1				11/20/13

Your Business
Main St
Yourtown USA

ASSETS	END OF Day 0	END OF Day 1	END OF year 1	END OF year 2	END OF year 3
CURRENT ASSETS					
Cash	303,550.00				
Inventory		20,000.00			
Accounts Receievable					
Supplies		15,550.00			
Rent Deposit		3,500.00			
Tel Deposit		400.00			
Util Deposit		1,200.00			
Misc equipment		3,100.00			
TOTAL CURRENT ASSETS	303,550.00	43,750.00	-	-	-
FIXED ASSETS					
Long Term Investments					
Property & Plant		5,000.00			
Goodwill					
Machinery & Equipment		250,000.00			
Less Depreciation (accumulated)					
TOTAL FIXED ASSETS	-	255,000.00	-	-	-
TOTAL ASSETS	303,550.00	298,750.00	-	-	-
LIABILITIES					
CURRENT LIABILITIES					
Bank loans (short-term)	20,000.00	20,000.00			
Wages Payable					
TOTAL CURRENT LIABILITIES	20,000.00	20,000.00	-	-	-
LONG-TERM LIABILITIES					
Bank Loans Payable	200,000.00	200,000.00			
Notes Payable					
TOTAL LONG-TERM LIABILITIES	200,000.00	200,000.00	-	-	-
TOTAL LIABILITIES	220,000.00	220,000.00	-	-	-
OWNERS' EQUITY					
Owners Capital	83,550.00	83,550.00			
Retained earnings		(4,800.00)			
TOTAL OWNERS' EQUITY	83,550.00	78,750.00	-	-	-
TOTAL LIABILITIES & OWNERS' EQUITY	303,550.00	298,750.00	-	-	-

Notes:

Assumptions:

The Statement of Shareholders' Equity

The Statement of Shareholders' Equity is a financial reporting document used to state changes in the shareholder' (owners') equity over a period of time, and to state the shareholder' equity position in the company at a particular point in time. Equity includes what the owners invested, retained earnings, and appreciation, less liabilities.

Shareholders' equity primarily comes from two sources; investment in the company and retained earnings from the operations of the company.

Typically, the first source of shareholders' equity is the initial money invested in the company by its founders. The second basic source of shareholders' equity comes from profit the company generates through its operations.

> **Statement of Changes in Shareholders' Equity (Statement of Owners' Equity)**
> - reports the changes in the shareholder' (owners) equity over a period of time
> - reports the shareholder' (owners) equity position in the company at a particular point in time

At the end of the accounting period, profit is accounted as retained earnings, or owners' equity.

Retained earnings are the undistributed profits the company generated during the prior accounting period, which becomes equity of the shareholders.

Accounting Equation: Statement of Changes in Shareholders' Equity
Owner's Equity = Beginning Owner's Equity + Investment by Owner + Net Income

---

Statement of Shareholders' Equity Worksheet

Date: _____
Name: _____
Business: _____

Statement of Shareholders' Equity
for the period ending   END OF PERIOD   7/1/14

Your Business
Main St
Yourtown USA

Beginning Equity	START of PERIOD
plus: Equity Investments	
plus: net income for	YEAR
less: Dividends for	YEAR
Ending Equity	END OF PERIOD $ -

Supplemental Financial Documents

Supplemental Financial Documents are intended to provide detail and explanations to line items on Financial Statements.

Develop and use Supplemental Financial Documents to provide the reader with insight and details into the development of line items on your Financial Statements.

Examples of some common Supplemental Financial Documents include:

Sources and Uses of Funds Statement
The Sources and Uses of Fund Statement provides a summary of where money is coming from, and where the money is going, as an easy-to-read, one-page reference.

Capital Equipment
The Capital Equipment document lists capital assets. Capital assets are assets that last longer than one year, can be depreciated, and are generally financed with long-term capital or are leased.

Start Up Costs (One-time Expenses)
The Start-Up Costs (One-time Expenses) statement is used to identify and list one-time (non-recurring) expenses.

Sales Estimates
The sales forecast should answer two key questions; how much do you plan on selling, and when will you sell it. Typically sales forecast provide a per unit quantity at a specific price, over a certain time frame.

Inventory
Maintaining adequate inventory levels of fresh and relevant products is important to assure customer availability while excess inventory can cash flow problems.

Operating Expenses
Operating expenses include all the day-to-day costs associated with operating the business. These are the costs associated with running the business and are seen on the Income Statement.

Wages/Salaries

Wages/Salaries documentation estimates project employee needs and hiring, along with associated costs. Wages are often one of the highest average expenses for a business.

Marketing and Promotional Expenses

Marketing and Promotional Expenses are use to report marketing communications and promotional activities and expenses.

Loan Repayments Schedules

Loan Repayment Schedules identify the repayment schedule of long and short-term loans.

Depreciation Schedules

The Depreciation Schedule is used to identify and list the depreciation of capital assets. Depreciation is an accounting and financial reporting practice that is used to reduce reported income and the resulting tax liabilities. Depreciation is a non-cash expense, and it is reported on the Income Statement.

Loan Application

A Loan Application is a form that is required by banks when you apply for a loan. These are available from the bank at which you request a loan. Obtain this form from your bank.

Term Sheet

A term sheet outlines the details of a proposed business agreement and they are often used as a preliminary step in negotiating an equity investment or transaction. A term sheet may or may not be legally binding.

Sources and Uses of Funds

The Sources and Uses of Fund statement is a simple yet important financial document for the banker. Essentially, the Sources and Uses of Funds statement provides the reader with a convenient synopsis of financing needs of the business.

The Sources and Uses of Fund statement provides a summary of where money is coming from, the type of money (debt or equity), and where it will be allocated, in an easy-to-read, one-page reference source.

> **Sources and Uses of Funds**
> - Identify and list all sources of funds required for the business including, short-term, long-term and equity investments
> - Identify and list all uses of funds within the business including start-up expenses, capital expenses, inventory, operating expenses, etc.
> - Provide an overview and reference of financing activities of the business
> - Provide a link between the text and financial statements

The statement allows the banker to quickly determine the financial needs of the business, determine from where the required funding is expected to be received and identify by category how the funds will be used.

Sources and Uses of Funds statement links the text of the business plan to the financial statements. Depending on the needs of the business, the Sources and Uses of Funds statement has the potential to be connected to virtually all text sections of the plan.

Sources and Uses of Funds Worksheet

Date: _____

Name: _____

Business: _____

Sources and Uses of Funds Statement Year 1 7/1/14

Your Business
Main St
Yourtown USA

Amount Requested: $ 200,000 Long-term loan   Line of Credit | $ 24,600 |
$ 20,000 Short-term loan
$ 220,000 **Total Amount Requested**

Purpose:

USE OF FUNDS SOURCE OF FUNDS

	Equity	Long-Term Loan	Short-Term Loan	Total
Capital Equipment	50,000	200,000		250,000
One Time Start up Costs	14,900			14,900
Misc Equipment	3,100			3,100
Supplies and Expenses	15,550			15,550
Inventory			20,000	20,000
				-
				-
				-
				-
TOTAL	$ 83,550	$ 200,000	$ 20,000	$ 303,550

Notes:

THE
BUSINESS PLAN
WORKBOOK

© E Clark 2014

The Business Plan Workbook

Capital Equipment

The Capital Equipment list is, as its name implies, simply a list of capital equipment. Capital assets are assets that last longer than one year and can be depreciated.

Capital Equipment List
• List and identify capital expenditures
• Itemize and tabulate capital expenses

Capital Equipment is generally financed with long-term capital or leased.

Use the Capital Equipment list to show the assets that you plan on acquiring with requested funding and to list assets that could potentially be used as collateral.

The major difference between the One-time Start-up Costs and One-time Expenses list and the Capital Equipment list is that the latter is comprised of capital assets; not expenses.

Capital Equipment
Worksheet

Date: _____

Name: _____

Business: _____

Capital Equipment List   7/1/14

Your Business
Main St
Yourtown USA

Total Capital Equipment: $ **250,000.00**

#	Item	Amount
1	Machines	50,000.00
2	Equipment	80,000.00
3	Trucks (4)	120,000.00
4		
5		
6		
7		
8		
9		
10		
11		
12		
13		
14		
15		
16		
17		
18		
19		
20		

Notes:

Start-up Costs & One-time Expenses

The Start-up Costs and One-time Expenses statement is used to identify and list One-time (non-recurring) Start-up Costs and Expenses associated with starting (or expanding) the business.

> **Start-up Costs and One-time Expenses**
> - Identify and list Start-up Costs and One-time Expenses
> - Itemize and tabulate Start-up Costs and One-time Expenses Provide an overview and reference of Start-up Costs and One-time Expenses activities of the business
> - Provide a link between the text and financial statements

The Start-up Costs and One-time Expenses statement is very straightforward; it is simply a list of items placed in appropriate categories. There is no set standard listing of categories. Develop categories for your list as appropriate to your business. Try to make the sections meaningful and so that they will make reading the financials and text easier.

Start-up Costs and One-time Expenses statement is not connected to the Capital Equipment list. Capital Equipment is listed separately to make calculating depreciation easier and as it is typically financed with long-term capital.

Start Up Costs & One Time Expenses
Worksheet

Date: _____

Name: _____

Business: _____

One Time Start up Costs and Expenses		7/1/14
Your Business		
Main St		
Yourtown USA		
Total Amount:	**$**	**53,550.00**
One Time Start up Costs		
1 Rent deposit		3,500.00
2 Telephone (deposit)		400.00
3 Utilities (deposits)		1,200.00
4 Rennovations (leashold)		5,000.00
5 Legal expenses		300.00
6 Accounting expenses		200.00
7 Opening expenses		1,200.00
8 Promotional expenses		2,500.00
9 License and Permits		600.00
10		
11		
12		
13		
14		
15		
	$	**14,900.00**
Misc Equipment		
16 Heat guns		400.00
17 cutters		250.00
18 gloves		200.00
19 racks		750.00
20 gps equipment		800.00
21 two-way radios		400.00
22 cell phones		300.00
23		
24		
25		
	$	**3,100.00**
Supplies and Expenses		
26 tape		200.00
27 adhesives		350.00
28 inventory		15,000.00
29		
30		
31		
32		
33		
34		
35		
	$	**15,550.00**
Inventory		
30 Glass		20,000.00
37		
38		
39		
40		
	$	**20,000.00**

THE BUSINESS PLAN WORKBOOK

© E Clark 2014

The Business Plan Workbook

Sales Estimates

The Sales Forecast is perhaps the most important estimate in a Business Plan. Virtually every other aspect of the business is connected to and based on the volume and timing of sales.

A sales forecast should answer two key questions; at a given price, how much will sell, and when will you sell it? A simple sales estimate will clearly provide and explain the Quantity x Price (by product/metric over a relevant time frame).

Sales estimates can be reported by any meaningful metric including department or division, sales person, geographic area, or by product. Additionally sales estimates can be reported in variety of timeframes, for example, weekly, monthly or quarterly.

In addition to providing the "numbers" it's critical to provide a clear explanation as to how the numbers were developed. Provide insight to all assumptions and references that were used to develop the sales estimates.

Sales estimates can be included in either the text section of the Business Plan or as part of the Supplemental Financial Documentation.

A key issue for the sales estimates is to provide a clear and logical explanation as to the methodology used to develop them. Numbers, by themselves, are just numbers.

Without a clear and compelling explanation as to how the numbers were developed they will be pointless. Numbers without an explanation are meaningless. For example if you based your sales estimates on historical financial data, past performance, industry averages or ratios it is important to say this and to provide the sources of your data.

For more detail on Sales Estimates Worksheets, see the Sales section of the Business Plan.

Sales Estimates
Worksheet

Date: _____

Name: _____

Business: _____

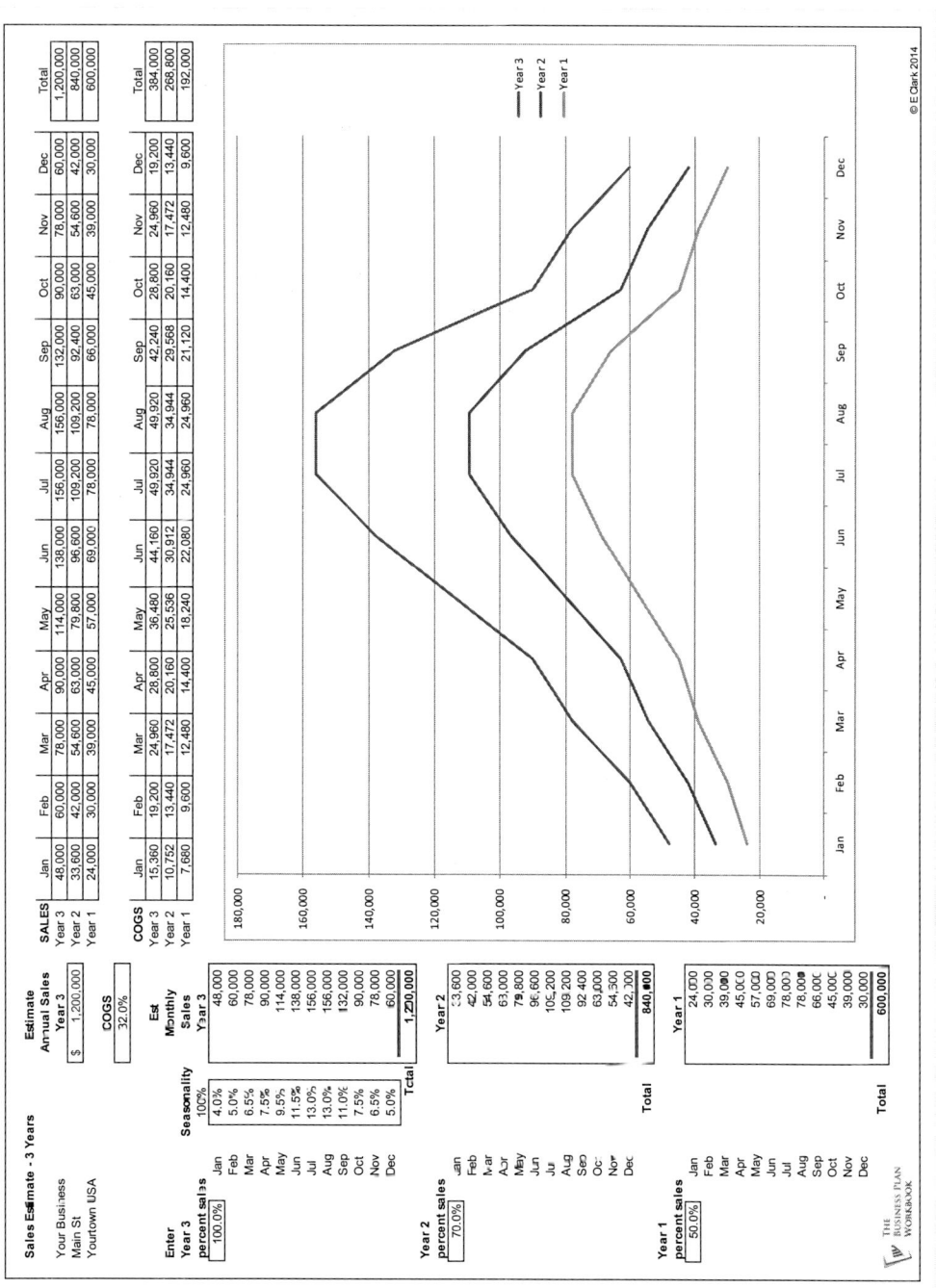

Inventory

Tracking Inventory and identifying the Cost of Goods Sold is critical to the financial health of business that manufactures products or is a reseller.

Maintaining adequate inventory levels of fresh and relevant products is important to assure customer availability while excess inventory can cash flow problems. Further excess inventory can add to carrying costs and increase the likelihood of spoilage or theft.

The basic formula to calculate Cost of Goods Sold (COGS) is:

$$
\begin{array}{ll}
 & \text{Beginning inventory} \\
+ & \text{additional inventory purchased} \\
- & \underline{\text{ending inventory}} \\
= & \text{COGS}
\end{array}
$$

For our purposes and the development of a pro forma the formula can also be changed to

$$
\begin{array}{ll}
 & \text{Beginning inventory} \\
+ & \text{additional inventory purchased} \\
- & \underline{\text{COGS}} \\
= & \text{ending inventory}
\end{array}
$$

If you have the average COGS as a reference from industry or historical data changing the formula is an effective method to identify inventory requirements.

For most businesses COGS is a variable expense. The more you sell the greater the COGS.

Most industries have a Metric that identifies the average percentage of COGS. If you are able to acquire a COGS metric for your business type, then developing the COGS should be fairly simple.

The trick here now and the hard part of developing Inventory requirements is to determine when inventory needs to be acquired and when payments to suppliers need to occur. These estimates can have a significant impact on cash flow requirements.

Inventory
Worksheet

Date: _____

Name: _____

Business: _____

Inventory   Year 1   7/1/14

Your Business
Main St
Yourtown USA

MONTH	Jan	Feb	Mar	Apr	May	Jun	Jul	Aug	Sep	Oct	Nov	Dec	TOTAL	%
Beginning Inventory	20,000	23,800	23,800	23,800	23,800	23,800	23,800	23,800	23,800	23,800	23,800	23,800	281,800	100%
1 Product 1	10,000	10,000	10,000	10,000	10,000	10,000	10,000	10,000	10,000	10,000	10,000	10,000	120,000	38.8%
2 Product 2	5,000	5,000	5,000	5,000	5,000	5,000	5,000	5,000	5,000	5,000	5,000	5,000	60,000	19.4%
3 Product 3	4,000	4,000	4,000	4,000	4,000	4,000	4,000	4,000	4,000	4,000	4,000	4,000	48,000	15.5%
4 Product 4	3,000	3,000	3,000	3,000	3,000	3,000	3,000	3,000	3,000	3,000	3,000	3,000	36,000	11.6%
5 Product 5	2,000	2,000	2,000	2,000	2,000	2,000	2,000	2,000	2,000	2,000	2,000	2,000	24,000	7.8%
6 Product 6	1,000	1,000	1,000	1,000	1,000	1,000	1,000	1,000	1,000	1,000	1,000	1,000	12,000	3.9%
7 Product 7	500	500	500	500	500	500	500	500	500	500	500	500	6,000	1.9%
8 Product 8	300	300	300	300	300	300	300	300	300	300	300	300	3,600	1.2%
Inventory Purchased	25,800	25,800	25,800	25,800	25,800	25,800	25,800	25,800	25,800	25,800	25,800	25,800	309,600	
Cost of Goods Sold	22,000	25,800	25,800	25,800	25,800	25,800	25,800	25,800	25,800	25,800	25,800	25,800	305,800	
Ending Inventory	23,800	23,800	23,800	23,800	23,800	23,800	23,800	23,800	23,800	23,800	23,800	23,800	285,600	

Notes:

Operating Expenses

Operating expenses include all the day-to-day costs associated with operating the business. These are the costs associated with running the business and are seen on the Income Statement.

Operating expenses include items such as:
- Wages and Salaries
- Rent
- Utilities, e.g., electricity, gas, water, sewage, telephone
- Sales, General and Administrative expenses
- Accounting expenses
- Legal expenses
- Marketing and Promotional expenses
- Insurance
- Auto Expenses
- Operating Supplies
- Repairs/ Maintenance
- Travel expenses

Operating Expenses are generally relatively fixed costs and do not vary directly with fluctuations in sales levels.

Some Operating Expenses such as wages and rent can account for major percentages of total costs. For example wages can be often be 30% of total costs when running a business

Fort larger expenses and or business critical issues such as Wages/Salaries, and Marketing and Promotional Expenses, greater detail should be provided as part of the development of your Business Plan and additional

Supplemental worksheets have been included for added detail.

Operating Expenses
Worksheet

Date: _____

Name: _____

Business: _____

Operating Expenses

Line
1 Wages - Salaries

MONTH	Jan	Feb	Mar	Apr	May	Jun	Jul	Aug	Sep	Oct	Nov	Dec	TOTAL	%
Year 1	10,440	10,440	10,440	13,920	13,920	13,920	13,920	13,920	13,920	13,920	13,920	13,920	156,600	26.10%
Year 2	13,920	13,920	13,920	24,312	24,312	24,312	24,312	24,312	17,400	17,400	17,400	17,400	232,920	27.73%
Year 3	17,400	17,400	17,400	27,792	27,792	27,792	27,792	27,792	20,880	20,880	20,880	20,880	274,680	22.89%

Line
2 Rent

MONTH	Jan	Feb	Mar	Apr	May	Jun	Jul	Aug	Sep	Oct	Nov	Dec	TOTAL	%
Year 1	2,800	2,800	2,800	2,800	2,800	2,800	2,800	2,800	2,800	2,800	2,800	2,800	33,600	5.60%
Year 2	2,800	2,800	2,800	2,800	2,800	2,800	2,800	2,800	2,800	2,800	2,800	2,800	33,600	4.00%
Year 3	2,800	2,800	2,800	2,800	2,800	2,800	2,800	2,800	2,800	2,800	2,800	2,800	33,600	2.80%

Line
3 Utilities, elec

MONTH	Jan	Feb	Mar	Apr	May	Jun	Jul	Aug	Sep	Oct	Nov	Dec	TOTAL	%
Year 1	2,800	2,800	2,800	2,800	2,800	2,800	2,800	2,800	2,800	2,800	2,800	2,800	33,600	5.60%
Year 2	3,200	3,200	3,200	3,200	3,200	3,200	3,200	3,200	3,200	3,200	3,200	3,200	38,400	4.57%
Year 3	3,400	3,400	3,400	3,400	3,400	3,400	3,400	3,400	3,400	3,400	3,400	3,400	40,800	3.40%

Line
4 Sales, General and Admin

MONTH	Jan	Feb	Mar	Apr	May	Jun	Jul	Aug	Sep	Oct	Nov	Dec	TOTAL	%
Year 1	1,800	1,800	1,800	1,800	1,800	1,800	1,800	1,800	1,800	1,800	1,800	1,800	21,600	3.60%
Year 2	2,200	2,200	2,200	2,200	2,200	2,200	2,200	2,200	2,200	2,200	2,200	2,200	26,400	3.14%
Year 3	2,600	2,600	2,600	2,600	2,600	2,600	2,600	2,600	2,600	2,600	2,600	2,600	31,200	2.60%

Line
5 Accounting / Legal

MONTH	Jan	Feb	Mar	Apr	May	Jun	Jul	Aug	Sep	Oct	Nov	Dec	TOTAL	%
Year 1	600	600	600	600	600	600	600	600	600	600	600	600	7,200	1.20%
Year 2	700	700	700	700	700	700	700	700	700	700	700	700	8,400	1.00%
Year 3	800	800	800	800	800	800	800	800	800	800	800	800	9,600	0.80%

Line
6 Mktg - Promotion

MONTH	Jan	Feb	Mar	Apr	May	Jun	Jul	Aug	Sep	Oct	Nov	Dec	TOTAL	%
Year 1	1,400	900	800	1,500	800	900	700	900	800	1,500	400	900	11,500	1.92%
Year 2	1,400	900	800	1,500	800	900	700	900	800	1,500	400	900	11,500	1.37%
Year 3	1,400	900	800	1,500	800	900	700	900	800	1,500	400	900	11,500	0.96%

Line
7 Insurance

MONTH	Jan	Feb	Mar	Apr	May	Jun	Jul	Aug	Sep	Oct	Nov	Dec	TOTAL	%
Year 1	900	900	900	900	900	900	900	900	900	900	900	900	10,800	1.80%
Year 2	1,200	1,200	1,200	1,200	1,200	1,200	1,200	1,200	1,200	1,200	1,200	1,200	14,400	1.71%
Year 3	1,500	1,500	1,500	1,500	1,500	1,500	1,500	1,500	1,500	1,500	1,500	1,500	18,000	1.50%

Line
8 Auto Expenses

MONTH	Jan	Feb	Mar	Apr	May	Jun	Jul	Aug	Sep	Oct	Nov	Dec	TOTAL	%
Year 1	900	900	900	900	900	900	900	900	900	900	900	900	10,800	1.80%
Year 2	1,400	1,400	1,400	1,400	1,400	1,400	1,400	1,400	1,400	1,400	1,400	1,400	16,800	2.00%
Year 3	1,800	1,800	1,800	1,800	1,800	1,800	1,800	1,800	1,800	1,800	1,800	1,800	21,600	1.80%

Line
9 L-T Loan

MONTH	Jan	Feb	Mar	Apr	May	Jun	Jul	Aug	Sep	Oct	Nov	Dec	TOTAL	%
Year 1	-	2,000	2,090	2,090	2,090	2,090	2,090	2,090	2,090	2,090	2,090	2,090	22,991	3.83%
Year 2	2,090	2,090	2,090	2,090	2,090	2,090	2,090	2,090	2,090	2,090	2,090	2,090	25,081	2.99%
Year 3	2,090	2,090	2,090	2,090	2,090	2,090	2,090	2,090	2,090	2,090	2,090	2,090	25,081	2.09%

Wages/Salaries

Wages/Salary estimates project employee needs and hiring along with associated costs.

For many businesses wages are one of highest, or the highest expenses.

Use this section to provide a detailed accounting for estimated expenses related to wages and employees.

Wages and salaries expenses are included as a line item on the Income Statement

For most businesses Wages is a relatively fixed expense. Minor fluctuations in sales generally have no effect on wages.

Wages/Salary Estimates Worksheet

Date: _____

Name: _____

Business: _____

Employee Wages and Salaries

Your Business
Main St
Yourtown USA

7/1/14

Year 1

	Jan	Feb	Mar	Apr	May	Jun	Jul	Aug	Sep	Oct	Nov	Dec	Total
Staff													
employees	1	1	1	2	2	2	2	2	2	2	2	2	
mo. wage	2,400.00	2,400.00	2,400.00	2,400.00	2,400.00	2,400.00	2,400.00	2,400.00	2,400.00	2,400.00	2,400.00	2,400.00	
ttl wages	2,400.00	2,400.00	2,400.00	4,800.00	4,800.00	4,800.00	4,800.00	4,800.00	4,800.00	4,800.00	4,800.00	4,800.00	
taxes/benefits 0.45	1,080.00	1,080.00	1,080.00	2,160.00	2,160.00	2,160.00	2,160.00	2,160.00	2,160.00	2,160.00	2,160.00	2,160.00	
Total Benefits & Wages	3,480.00	3,480.00	3,480.00	6,960.00	6,960.00	6,960.00	6,960.00	6,960.00	6,960.00	6,960.00	6,960.00	6,960.00	
Line													
employees	2	2	2	2	2	2	2	2	2	2	2	2	
mo. wage	2,400.00	2,400.00	2,400.00	2,400.00	2,400.00	2,400.00	2,400.00	2,400.00	2,400.00	2,400.00	2,400.00	2,400.00	
ttl wages	4,800.00	4,800.00	4,800.00	4,800.00	4,800.00	4,800.00	4,800.00	4,800.00	4,800.00	4,800.00	4,800.00	4,800.00	
taxes/benefits 0.45	2,160.00	2,160.00	2,160.00	2,160.00	2,160.00	2,160.00	2,160.00	2,160.00	2,160.00	2,160.00	2,160.00	2,160.00	
Total Benefits & Wages	6,960.00	6,960.00	6,960.00	6,960.00	6,960.00	6,960.00	6,960.00	6,960.00	6,960.00	6,960.00	6,960.00	6,960.00	
Part-time													
employees	-	2		2	2	2	2	2	-	-	-	-	
hourly pay	12												
hours per month	-	-	-	120	120	120	120	120	-	-	-	-	
ttl wages	-	-	-	-	-	-	-	-	-	-	-	-	
taxes/benefits 0.20	-	-	-	-	-	-	-	-	-	-	-	-	
Total Benefits & Wages	-	-	-	-	-	-	-	-	-	-	-	-	
Total Wages/Salaries	10,440.00	10,440.00	10,440.00	13,920.00	13,920.00	13,920.00	13,920.00	13,920.00	13,920.00	13,920.00	13,920.00	13,920.00	156,600.00

Marketing and Promotional Expenses

Marketing and Promotional Expenses are used to report marketing communications and promotional activities and expenses. Every business needs to drive sales through marketing.

Develop a comprehensive promotional campaign strategy and provide documentation and details regarding activities and costs.

Marketing and Promotional Expenses are a line item on the Income Statement.

Marketing - Promotional Expenses Worksheet

Date: _____

Name: _____

Business: _____

Promotion/Marketing Mix

Your Business
Main St
Yourtown USA

7/1/14

Promotion	Jan	Feb	Mar	Apr	May	Jun	Jul	Aug	Sep	Oct	Nov	Dec	Total
sponsorship	400.00		400.00		400.00				400.00				
product placement													
endorsements													
merchandising	100.00	100.00	100.00	100.00	100.00	100.00	100.00	100.00	100.00	100.00	100.00	100.00	
public relations													
trade shows													
Advertising													
TV	600.00			600.00			600.00			600.00			
radio		500.00				500.00		500.00					
newspapers				500.00						500.00		500.00	
Internet	300.00	300.00	300.00	300.00	300.00	300.00		300.00	300.00	300.00	300.00	300.00	
Mobile Phones													
	1,400.00	900.00	800.00	1,500.00	800.00	900.00	700.00	900.00	800.00	1,500.00	400.00	900.00	**11,500.00**

© E Clark 2014

Notes and assumptions:

THE BUSINESS PLAN WORKBOOK

Loan Repayment Schedules

Loan Repayment Schedules identify the repayment schedule of long and short-term loans.

Itemize short-term and long-term loan repayment, including interest expenses.

While interest can be deducted as an expense on the Income Statement, principal for Loan Repayments is typically not seen as an operating expense.

For the development of pro forma financial statements it is acceptable to include loan repayments on the Income Statement.

These payments will be seen on the cash flow Statement.

Loan Repayment Schedule Worksheet

Date: _____
Name: _____
Business: _____

Short-Term Loan Repayment Schedule

7/1/14

Year 1	Loan 1 Jan	Loan 2 Feb	Loan 3 Mar	Loan 4 Apr	Loan 5 May	Loan 6 Jun	Loan 7 Jul	Loan 8 Aug	Loan 9 Sep	Loan 10 Oct	Loan 11 Nov	Loan 12 Dec	
Start-Up S-T Loan	20,000												**Total Debt**
Amount Borrowed	11,200	9,400	4,000										$ 24,600.00
	31,200.00												
interest rate	0.06	0.06	0.06	0.06	0.06	0.06	0.06	0.06	0.06	0.06	0.06	0.06	
term-months	12	12	12	12	12	12	12	12	12	12	12	12	
interest exp	1,872	564	240	-	-	-	-	-	-	-	-	-	47,276
total	33,072	9,964	4,240	-	-	-	-	-	-	-	-	-	
payment (simple)	2,756.00	830.33	353.33	-	-	-	-	-	-	-	-	-	
Payments Loan 1		2,755.00	2,756.00	2,756.00	2,756.00	2,756.00	2,756.00	2,756.00	2,756.00	2,756.00	2,756.00	2,756.00	**Includes Start-up**
Loan 2			830.33	830.33	830.33	830.33	830.33	830.33	830.33	830.33	830.33	830.33	
Loan 3				353.33	353.33	353.33	353.33	353.33	353.33	353.33	353.33	353.33	
Loan 4					-	-	-	-	-	-	-	-	
Loan 5						-	-	-	-	-	-	-	
Loan 6							-	-	-	-	-	-	
Loan 7								-	-	-	-	-	
Loan 8									-	-	-	-	**Outstanding**
Loan 9										-	-	-	**Balance Due**
Loan 10											-	-	$ 5,476.67
Loan 11												-	
Loan 12													
Total Loan Payment	-	2,755	3,586	3,940	3,940	3,940	3,940	3,940	3,940	3,940	3,940	3,940	41,799.33

The Business Plan Workbook

Depreciation Schedule

Depreciation is an accounting and financial reporting practice that is used to reduce reported income and the resulting tax liabilities.

The intent of depreciation is to provide the business owner with tax benefits for capital equipment and investments that have a useful life and wear out over a period of time

Generally assets can be depreciated if they have a useful life of greater than one year, are used in the business and are expected to become obsolete or wear out over time from normal use.

Depreciation is a non-cash expense, and it is reported on the Income Statement.

Depreciation Schedule Worksheet

Date: _____
Name: _____
Business: _____

Depreciation Schedules

Your Business
Main St
Yourtown USA

7/1/14

Year 1

Asset	Book Value	depr. term mos.	Jan	Feb	Mar	Apr	May	Jun	Jul	Aug	Sep	Oct	Nov	Dec
asset 1 (identify)	480,000	100	4,800	4,800.00	4,800.00	4,800.00	4,800.00	4,800.00	4,800.00	4,800.00	4,800.00	4,800.00	4,800.00	4,800.00
asset 2 (identify)	-	-												
asset 3 (identify)	-	-												
asset 4 (identify)	-	-												
asset 5 (identify)	-	-												
asset 6 (identiy)	-	-												
Total Monthly Depreciation			4,800.00	4,800.00	4,800.00	4,800.00	4,800.00	4,800.00	4,800.00	4,800.00	4,800.00	4,800.00	4,800.00	4,800.00	57,600.00

Year 2

Asset	Book Value	depr. term mos.	Jan	Feb	Mar	Apr	May	Jun	Jul	Aug	Sep	Oct	Nov	Dec
asset 1 (identify)			4,800	4,800	4,800	4,800	4,800	4,800	4,800	4,800	4,800	4,800	4,800	4,800
asset 2 (identify)			-	-	-	-	-	-	-	-	-	-	-	-
asset 3 (identify			-	-	-	-	-	-	-	-	-	-	-	-
asset 4 (identify			-	-	-	-	-	-	-	-	-	-	-	-
asset 5 (identify)			-	-	-	-	-	-	-	-	-	-	-	-
asset 6 (identify)			-	-	-	-	-	-	-	-	-	-	-	-
Total Monthly Depreciation			4,800.00	4,800.00	4,800.00	4,800.00	4,800.00	4,800.00	4,800.00	4,800.00	4,800.00	4,800.00	4,800.00	4,800.00	57,600.00

Year 3

Asset	Book Value	depr. term mos.	Jan	Feb	Mar	Apr	May	Jun	Jul	Aug	Sep	Oct	Nov	Dec
asset 1 (identify)			4,800	4,800	4,800	4,800	4,800	4,800	4,800	4,800	4,800	4,800	4,800	4,800
asset 2 (identify)			-	-	-	-	-	-	-	-	-	-	-	-
asset 3 (identify)			-	-	-	-	-	-	-	-	-	-	-	-
asset 4 (identify)			-	-	-	-	-	-	-	-	-	-	-	-
asset 5 (identify)			-	-	-	-	-	-	-	-	-	-	-	-
asset 6 (identify)			-	-	-	-	-	-	-	-	-	-	-	-
Total Monthly Depreciation			4,300.00	4,800.00	4,800.00	4,800.00	4,800.00	4,800.00	4,800.00	4,800.00	4,800.00	4,800.00	4,800.00	4,800.00	57,600.00

Notes and assumptions:

The Business Plan Workbook

Loan Application

Generally, when you apply for a loan the bank that you are requesting the loan from will require you to fill out a loan application.

Depending on the bank, the application may either be on-line or paper. Most banks ask for the same basic types of information.

Before you apply for a loan, call the bank and ask for the required paperwork.

They will be specific with what they want, and you should provide them with everything requested.

Do not submit your application materials piecemeal. Your application should be submitted as a completed package.

Loan Application
Worksheet

Date: _____

Name: _____

Business: _____

Commerce Bank
Commercial Loan Application

Contact Information
Business Name
Address
CSZ

Purpose of the Loan:

Amount requested:

Business Information:

Collateral:

Business Plan:

Term Sheet (For Equity Investments)

A term sheet is a document that outlines the details of a proposed business agreement.

Term sheets are often used as a preliminary step in negotiating an equity investment in a business.

A term sheet is used to identify issues and conditions in a business negotiation as part of an equity investment. A term sheet may or may not be legally binding.

For an Equity Investment in a business a typical term sheet would identify issues including, the Company Name, the Names and Contact Information of the Parties to the Agreement; the Purpose of the Agreement and key issues such as the Amount to be Invested and the Percentage of Ownership to be received in return for the Investment.

Additional items that should be considered in a term sheet may include: payments of Dividends, Valuation of the Company, and distributions in the event of liquidation.

This term sheets is for discussion purposes only and it does not impose any legally binding obligations on behalf of the associated parties.

Term Sheet
Worksheet

Date: _____

Name: _____

Business: _____

Term Sheet

Company Name:

Names and Contact Information of the Parties to the Agreement:

Purpose of this Agreement:

Terms
- Investment Amount
- Ownership Percentage

Confidentiality:

Non-Compete:

Duration of the agreement:

Dividends:

Valuation of the Company:

Liquidation:

The Business Plan Workbook

Supporting Documents/Appendix

The third section of the Business Plan is the **Supporting Documents and Appendixes**.

This section is used to provide any required backup materials and documentation for the reader

The Supporting Documents section provides a location for supporting documentation to create a package that is more easily read.

Provide relevant:
- Equipment Lists and Cut Sheets
- Personal Resumes
- Personal Financial Documentation
- Leases
- Licenses
- Contracts
- Supplier Lists
- Maps
- Facility layouts
- Other Relevant Documentation

Supporting documentation should be referenced to the appropriate sections in the business plan in which it is discussed

Chapter 4   Presenting Your Business Plan

Prepare Before Approach

Know Your Business

Know Your Audience

Your Presentation

Presentation Guidelines

Moving Ahead

Chapter 4

Presenting Your Business Plan

Prepare Before Approach

You've spent a lot of time and hard work developing a Business Plan and you're getting ready to put your best foot forward and present your business opportunity to a prospective lender. But before you make an appointment, take some time to prepare for your meeting and presentation. As with many things in life, preparation is half the battle.

Know Your Business

Be fully prepared to answer key questions about the financials for your business. For example, what are the margins, COGS, what are the expenses for your business, and what products drive revenues?

> **Prepare Before Approach**
>
> **Know Your Business**
> • The Financials
> • The Opportunity
> • Your Strategy
> • Your Tactics
>
> **Know Your Audience**
> • Qualify Them
> • Qualify Yourself
> • Create Desire
> • Create Action

Be prepared to discuss the opportunity you are presenting. What is the opportunity that makes your business attractive? Is there something special about the market or the situation is of particular interest? Be prepared to discuss how you will capture this opportunity. Be prepared to discuss your strategy to capture sales as well as specific tactics that you think will make your business successful.

Know Your Audience

Before you approach a prospective lender you should do some due diligence to assess if they are an appropriate prospect. Most lenders have some preferred business types, size, locations or industries in which they like to do business.

Many will not venture out of their comfort zone. Even if they think what you are doing is great, they will often pass if it's not in their preferred lending area. You want to know their lending abilities, criteria, and appetite before spending too much time pitching to them. It's perfectly acceptable to be direct and ask questions. Remember, they are in the business of lending. They want to lend money. It's what they do. They appreciate that you're being to the point. It shows them that you know what you want and what you are doing, which saves them time. As they are sizing up your ability to operate the business, you should be sizing them up to determine if they are an appropriate funding source. This is referred to as 'qualifying the banker.'

Qualifying means that you are trying to determine three things. You want to make certain that the lender is **ready**, **willing** and **able**. Are they **ready** to do the deal with you? Are they **willing** to do the deal with you?, And are they **able** to do the deal with you? .If they fall short on any one of these three criteria, you will not be able to accomplish your goal of getting funding.

As you are qualifying a lender, remember that they are qualifying you. They will be accessing that you are really ready, willing, and perhaps most importantly, able to achieve your business goals. What they want is for you to show them that you are a qualified creditor, and that you will pay them back. You need to assure them that you are also ready, willing, and able.

You also need to create desire and action. If you have shown them a suitable business opportunity, and both you and they are qualified, it is time to create action. This is when you get them to process the loan.

Your Presentation

Your presentation is a very important part of the funding process. This is about more than just a simple presentation; this is an opportunity for the lender to learn about your business, and perhaps more importantly, about you.

Your Presentation

Introduction
Discuss the Opportunity
Describe the Business
Close the Deal - Next Steps

The presentation itself can be broken down into four parts. An introduction, a discussion of the opportunity, a description of the business, and an attempt to close the deal and/or move on to the next steps.

A banker or investor wants to know about your business, but they also want to see you in action. This is an opportunity for them to evaluate you. You must realize that it is as much about you, as it is the business. You need to put on a good show. As you do this, consider some guideline to help you present more effectively.

Presentation Guidelines

When you met with the lender to discuss your business, stay on target. Keep your mission in mind and stay focused on what you need to do to achieve your goal. You can be relaxed and have fun, but in the end, this is about business, so stay on target.

Presentation Guidelines

• Stay On Target
• Start with General Information
• Focus on Key Issues
• Provide the Right Level of Detail
• Answer Questions with Specifics When Asked
• Always Be Closing

During your discussion and presentation, start with general information. Avoid details that bog down the discussion with technicalities or too fine a focus. Stay with general "big picture" issues and let the lender ask questions where they have them. If they have done their homework and have read your Business Plan beforehand, they will get to where they want to go with specific questions.

Focus on the key issues. Do not address issues that are not important. This shows the banker that you know what is important. Part of this focus is to provide the right level of detail. For example, you don't need to discuss all the elements of the Income Statement, just the key financial issues of importance, e.g., COGS and margins, your sales forecast.

Focus on the financial issues that are of importance to the banker.

Make certain that you address the key questions: How much money do you need? Be specific, short-term, long-term, line of credit. What are you going to do with the money? Again, be specific. Let them know when you will need it and for how long? Key to the presentation is, how you will pay them back? What they ideally want to see is that the business has the capacity and positive cash flow to cover the loan. They would also like you to discuss how you will minimize their risk with an assurance of collateral.

Provide Detail – The Right Level

- Sales Forecast
- COGS
- Variable Costs
- Margins
- Where the big money is going
- Where the returns are coming from

While it's good to stay focused on higher-level issues when you are asked a question, you should answer it with specifics. Try to answer the question with the right level of detail to address any concern. This is an opportunity to clarify what may be a problem and to show the lender that you understand the details of the business.

The presentation is more than just a discussion of your business. The presentation should be used for closing the deal. The presentation is essentially a sales call. As you present, your larger goal is to secure a loan, and as you go through your presentation, remember the ABC's of sales: Always Be Closing.

Before you begin your presentation, you should be aware of time. Find out how much time you will be given and adjust your presentation accordingly. Keep in mind that the presentation is for their benefit, not yours. Base what you are going to do and say on how much time you are allotted and make certain that you address their concerns and answer their questions.

Introduction

The Introduction should be brief and relaxed. Thank the lender for their time – remember they are doing you a favor, and you want something from them. Be direct and specific. Tell them exactly why you are there, what you want, and what you hope will happen at the meeting. If you've done a good job to qualify them, this will simply reestablish the purpose of the meeting.

Introduction

- Thank You
- Introduce Yourself
- Make a Connection
- Why You Are Here
  - Your Elevator Pitch
  - What Do You Want?
  - *Briefly* address the Readers **Basic Questions**

Qualify The Opportunity, the Deal, the Banker

What they want to know is some specifics and they generally have five basic questions they want answered, and answered quickly: How much money do you need? What are you going to do with the money? When do you need it and for how long? How will you pay me back? How can you assure me that I will get my money back? Get this to them quickly and move on to more information about you and the business.

Give them an elevator pitch about the business. In a few short sentences tell them, *what* your business sells, the (Product/Service). Tell them *who* your customers are, (Customer/Segment) and the *benefits* (value proposition) your customers receive. Tell them how you make the products available to your customers (*delivery*). Tell them how you are different, and why/how you will succeed. Sell them on what you do.

Discuss the Opportunity

Discuss What You Want The Banker To Know About the Opportunity
- What You Are Doing?
- Your Industry
- Your Business
- Your Customers
- Your Competitors
- Discuss What the Banker Needs to Know
- Discuss What You Want the Banker to Know

Discuss the Opportunity

Start with an overview of the opportunity. This section should build and expand on the elevator pitch with additional details. The main objective here is to create a high level visualization of the entire opportunity and business. A goal here is to answer basic questions and to frame the discussion for the next section of the presentation where additional detail will be added.

One objective here is to identify areas of interest or concern of the banker. This section of the presentation should be fairly brief.

Discuss The Business

- What Makes Your Company Special
  - Value Proposition
  - Your Product, Operations, Distribution
- Discuss your Customer/Segment
- Discuss your Competitors
- Discuss Your Marketing & Sales Plan
- Discuss Your Finances

Discuss the Business

This is the main part of the presentation and where details should be provided. The trick here is to provide answers to questions, but not get bogged down in minutia. Try to identify what the audience thinks is important and address those issues. This is about answering their questions and addressing their concerns, with a goal of getting them to lend you money. This is not about just discussing your business.

Issues to consider in this discussion include: What makes your company special? What the value is that you provide to your customers? How do you create value in your product? In your business operations?

Provide the Right Level of Detail

For Each Piece of Your Presentation
- Where the big money is going
- Where the returns are coming from
- Sales Forecast
- COGS
- Variable Costs
- Margins

Segment the presentation to include all relevant aspects of your business including: your Customer/Segment, your Competitors, your Marketing and Sales Plan, and your Finances.

For each section of your presentation, identify any money that you are investing or borrowing and what you are doing with that money. Discuss key financial aspects as you go through the sections and provide financial information, such as Sales Forecast, COGS, Variable Costs, and Margins. Again, the trick here is to provide answers to questions, without getting bogged down in minutia. Identify the important issues and focus on them.

Close the Deal - Next Steps

Don't blink now, close the deal. This is the whole reason you went through this process. Be direct, restate the opportunity and tell them what you want. Ask them for confirmation to move forward and close the Deal.

Close The Deal - Next Steps

• **Restate the Opportunity**
  – What you are doing
  – What you want
  – What's in it for them
• **Ask for what you want from them**
• *Ask for a Conformation to Move Forward*
  – Next Steps
• **Thank them for their time**

Close the Deal

If the lender presents objections or obstacles consider these as opportunities. Ask them if you can address and clarify or resolve those issues, and if that is that all that's needed to move forward. Get them to tell you what you need to do to come to an agreement. They want you to address their objections in order to move forward, so find out what you need to do to meet their expectations.

Going to the Bank

At this point, when you are going to the bank, you should be well prepared.

Going to the Bank

• Be Prepared
• Have an Appointment
• Prepare the Banker
• Show Up On Time
• Be Professional

You've written a great Business Plan, and crafted a great presentation. You've qualified yourself to the banker and you've qualified the banker for your needs. Everything should be set to go. The banker should now know you and what you want and you're ready to set an appointment. Ask them if they would like to have a copy of your business plan to read in advance of your meeting. That will help them to prepare and consider any questions that they might have for you.

Ask the banker if there is anything else that they can think of that they need from you. At this point you should be focused on to removing any and all obstacles that may prevent you from receiving a loan and moving forward.

Moving Ahead

At the end of your presentation you should have a very clear understanding of what will happen next. If there is any uncertainty on your end, you should ask questions. Usually, a lender will not provide a loan confirmation on the spot, but you should have a very clear understanding of what will happen next. If they seem positive about the loan, ask what their process is for approvals and generally how long it should take. Find out if there is anything that they need you to do for them.

You should feel comfortable with what they need and what they are dong. If you have any questions you should feel comfortable asking. If all goes well you will likely be establishing a long-term working relationship with the bank and you want things to go smoothly. So ask questions. Good luck.

Financial Worksheet Templates

Contact Data
Sources and Uses of Funds Statement
Capital Equipment
Start-Up Expenses

Sales Estimates
Sales Est - 1 year
Sales Est - 3 year
Sales Est - by Product

Financial Statements
Income Statement
Cash-Flow Statement
Balance Sheet
Statement of Shareholders' Equity

Supplemental Financial Documents
Operating Expenses
    Rent
    Utilities, elec., etc
    Sales, General and Admin
    Accounting / Legal
    Insurance
    Auto Expenses
    Operating Supplies
    Repairs/ Maintenance
Wages/Salaries
Inventory
Marketing - Promotional Expenses
Loan Repayment Schedule (short-term)
Loan Repayment Schedule (long-term)
Depreciation Schedules

Analysis Tools
Operating Ratios
Break Even Statement

For a complete set of linked excel Financial Templates visit:

www.TheBusinessPlanWorkbook.com

THE
BUSINESS PLAN
WORKBOOK

Contact Information

			Date
Business Plan		**Writer**	7/1/14
	Your Business	Name	
	Main St	Address	
	Yourtown USA	C, S, Z	

Business Principle 1

name	Joe Small
address 1	West St
CSZ	Yourtown USA
phone	
email	

Business Principle 2

name	
address 1	
address 2	
CSZ	
phone	
email	

Business Principle 3

name	
address 1	
address 2	
CSZ	
phone	
email	

Notes:

THE
BUSINESS PLAN
WORKBOOK

Sources and Uses of Funds Statement

Sources and Uses of Funds Statement	Year 1	7/1/14

Your Business
Main St
Yourtown USA

Amount Requested:

$	200,000	Long-term loan	Line of Credit	$ 24,600
$	20,000	Short-term loan		
$	220,000	**Total Amount Requested**		

Purpose:

USE OF FUNDS	SOURCE OF FUNDS			
	Equity	Long-Term Loan	Short-Term Loan	Total
Capital Equipment	50,000	200,000		250,000
One Time Start up Costs	14,900			14,900
Misc Equipment	3,100			3,100
Supplies and Expenses	15,550			15,550
Inventory			20,000	20,000
				-
				-
				-
				-
				-
TOTAL	$ 83,550	$ 200,000	$ 20,000	$ 303,550

Notes:

Financial Worksheet Templates

Capital Equipment

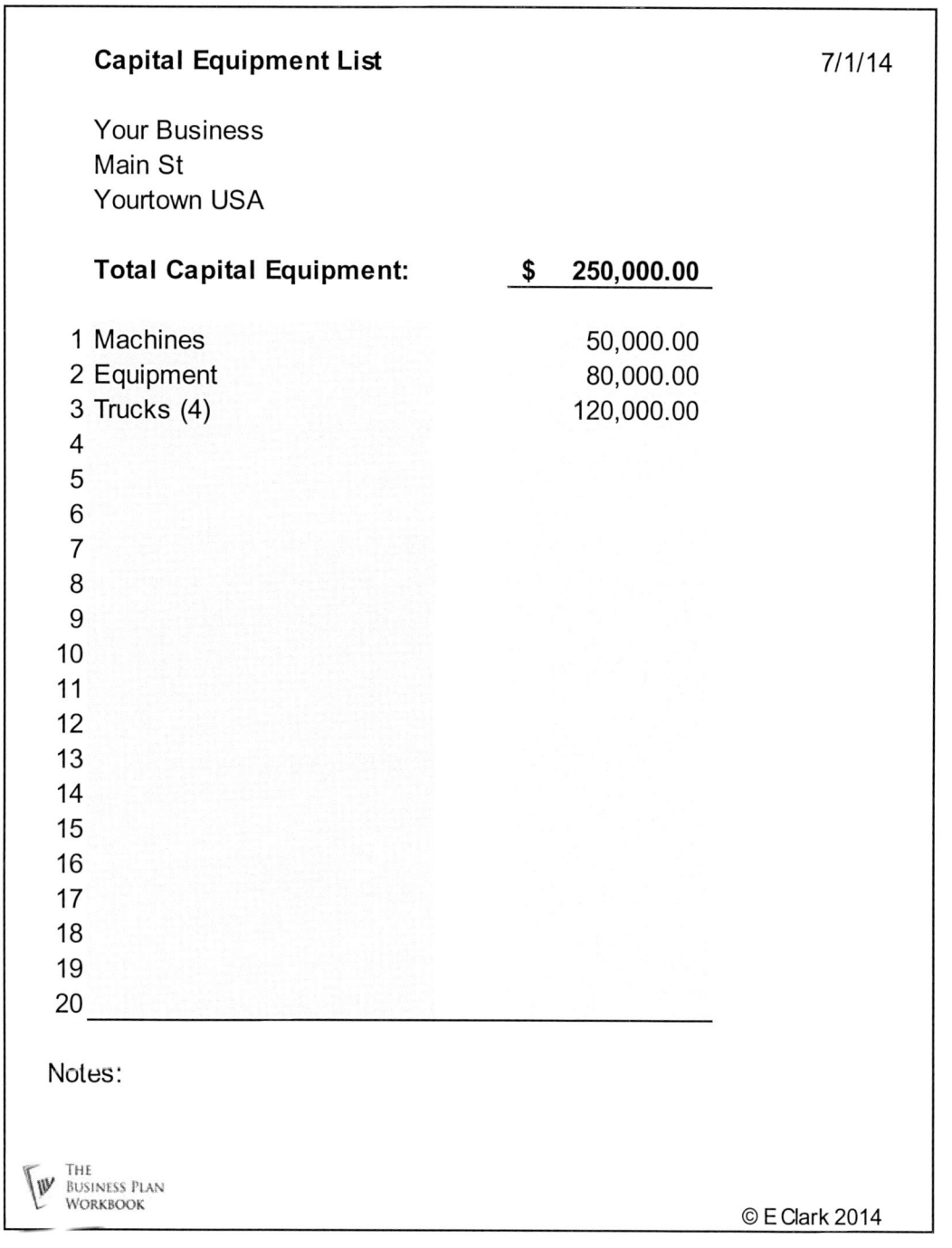

Capital Equipment List   7/1/14

Your Business
Main St
Yourtown USA

Total Capital Equipment: $ 250,000.00

1	Machines	50,000.00
2	Equipment	80,000.00
3	Trucks (4)	120,000.00
4		
5		
6		
7		
8		
9		
10		
11		
12		
13		
14		
15		
16		
17		
18		
19		
20		

Notes:

THE
BUSINESS PLAN
WORKBOOK

© E Clark 2014

The Business Plan Workbook

Start-Up Expenses

One Time Start up Costs and Expenses		7/1/14
Your Business		
Main St		
Yourtown USA		
Total Amount:	$	**53,550.00**
One Time Start up Costs		
1 Rent deposit		3,500.00
2 Telephone (deposit)		400.00
3 Utilities (deposits)		1,200.00
4 Rennovations (leashold)		5,000.00
5 Legal expenses		300.00
6 Accounting expenses		200.00
7 Opening expenses		1,200.00
8 Promotional expenses		2,500.00
9 License and Permits		600.00
10		
11		
12		
13		
14		
15		
	$	14,900.00
Misc Equipment		
16 Heat guns		400.00
17 cutters		250.00
18 gloves		200.00
19 racks		750.00
20 gps equipment		800.00
21 two-way radios		400.00
22 cell phones		300.00
23		
24		
25		
	$	3,100.00
Supplies and Expenses		
26 tape		200.00
27 adhesives		350.00
28 inventory		15,000.00
29		
30		
31		
32		
33		
34		
35		
	$	15,550.00
Inventory		
36 Glass		20,000.00
37		
38		
39		
40		
	$	20,000.00

THE
BUSINESS PLAN
WORKBOOK

© E Clark 2014

Financial W

Sales Estimates - 3 Years

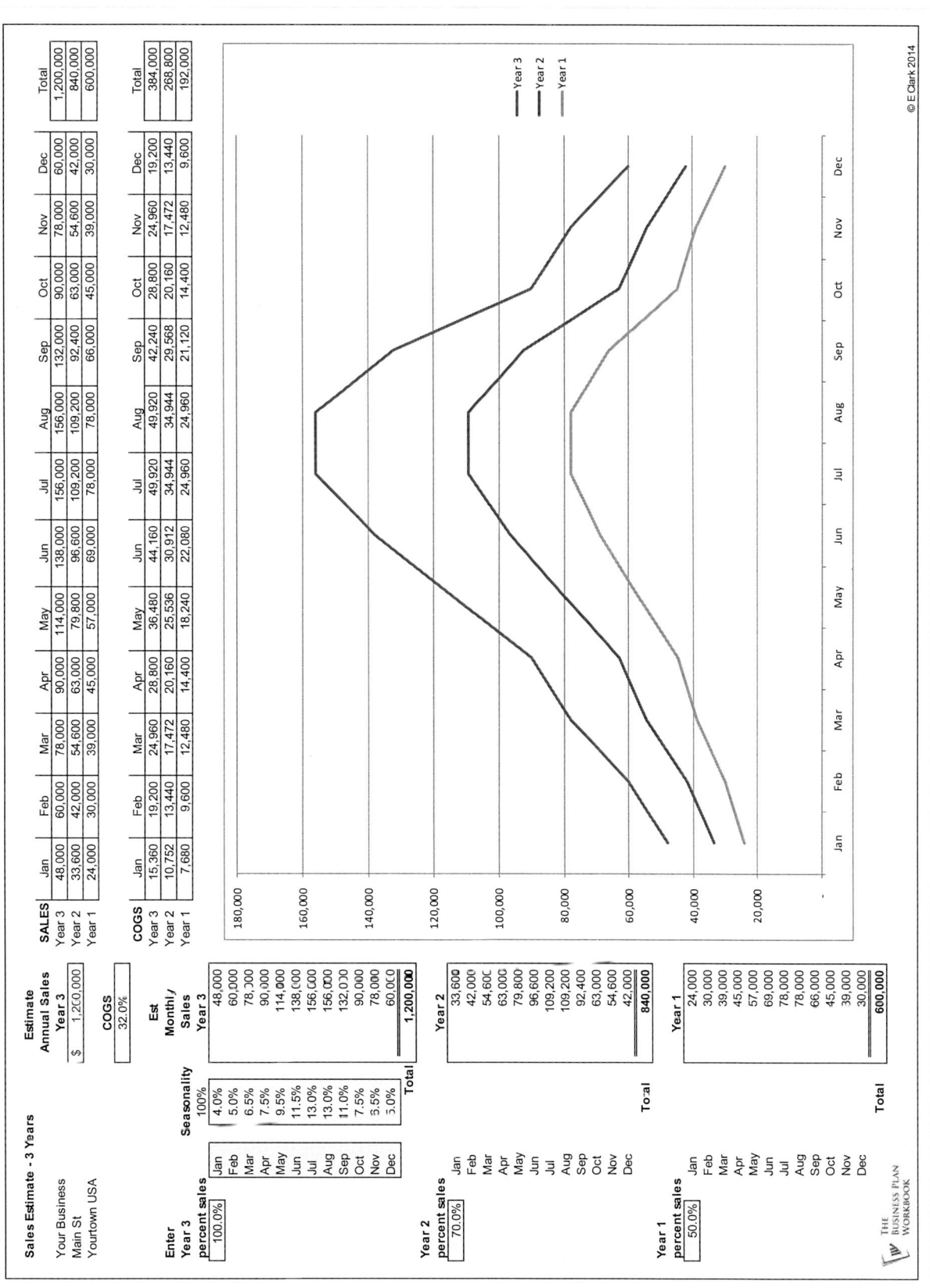

SALES	Jan	Feb	Mar	Apr	May	Jun	Jul	Aug	Sep	Oct	Nov	Dec	Total
Year 3	48,000	60,000	78,000	90,000	114,000	138,000	156,000	156,000	132,000	90,000	78,000	60,000	1,200,000
Year 2	33,600	42,000	54,600	63,000	79,800	96,600	109,200	109,200	92,400	63,000	54,600	42,000	840,000
Year 1	24,000	30,000	39,000	45,000	57,000	69,000	78,000	78,000	66,000	45,000	39,000	30,000	600,000

COGS	Jan	Feb	Mar	Apr	May	Jun	Jul	Aug	Sep	Oct	Nov	Dec	Total
Year 3	15,360	19,200	24,960	28,800	36,480	44,160	49,920	49,920	42,240	28,800	24,960	19,200	384,000
Year 2	10,752	13,440	17,472	20,160	25,536	30,912	34,944	34,944	29,568	20,160	17,472	13,440	268,800
Year 1	7,680	9,600	12,480	14,400	18,240	22,080	24,960	24,960	21,120	14,400	12,480	9,600	192,000

Sales Estimate - 3 Years

Your Business
Main St
Yourtown USA

Estimate Annual Sales Year 3	$ 1,200,000
COGS	32.0%

Enter Year 3 percent sales: 100.0%

	Seasonality 100%	Est Monthly Sales Year 3
Jan	4.0%	48,000
Feb	5.0%	60,000
Mar	6.5%	78,000
Apr	7.5%	90,000
May	9.5%	114,000
Jun	11.5%	138,000
Jul	13.0%	156,000
Aug	13.0%	156,000
Sep	11.0%	132,000
Oct	7.5%	90,000
Nov	6.5%	78,000
Dec	5.0%	60,000
Total		1,200,000

Year 2 percent sales: 70.0%

	Year 2
Jan	33,600
Feb	42,000
Mar	54,600
Apr	63,000
May	79,800
Jun	96,600
Jul	109,200
Aug	109,200
Sep	92,400
Oct	63,000
Nov	54,600
Dec	42,000
Total	840,000

Year 1 percent sales: 50.0%

	Year 1
Jan	24,000
Feb	30,000
Mar	39,000
Apr	45,000
May	57,000
Jun	69,000
Jul	78,000
Aug	78,000
Sep	66,000
Oct	45,000
Nov	39,000
Dec	30,000
Total	600,000

© E Clark 2014

Sales Estimates – 1 Year

	Jan	Feb	Mar	Apr	May	Jun	Jul	Aug	Sep	Oct	Nov	Dec	Total
SALES	48,000	60,000	78,000	90,000	114,000	138,000	156,000	156,000	132,000	90,000	78,000	60,000	1,200,000
COGS	15,360	19,200	24,960	28,800	36,480	44,160	49,920	49,920	42,240	28,800	24,960	19,200	384,000

Sales Estimate - 1 Year

Your Business
Main St
Yourtown USA

	Estimate Annual Sales
	$ 1,200,000

COGS
32.0%

Enter
Year 1
percent sales 100.0%

	Seasonality	Est Monthly Sales Year 3
	100%	
Jan	4.0%	48,000
Feb	5.0%	60,000
Mar	6.5%	78,000
Apr	7.5%	90,000
May	9.5%	114,000
Jun	11.5%	138,000
Jul	13.0%	156,000
Aug	13.0%	156,000
Sep	11.0%	132,000
Oct	7.5%	90,000
Nov	6.5%	78,000
Dec	5.0%	60,000
Total		1,200,000

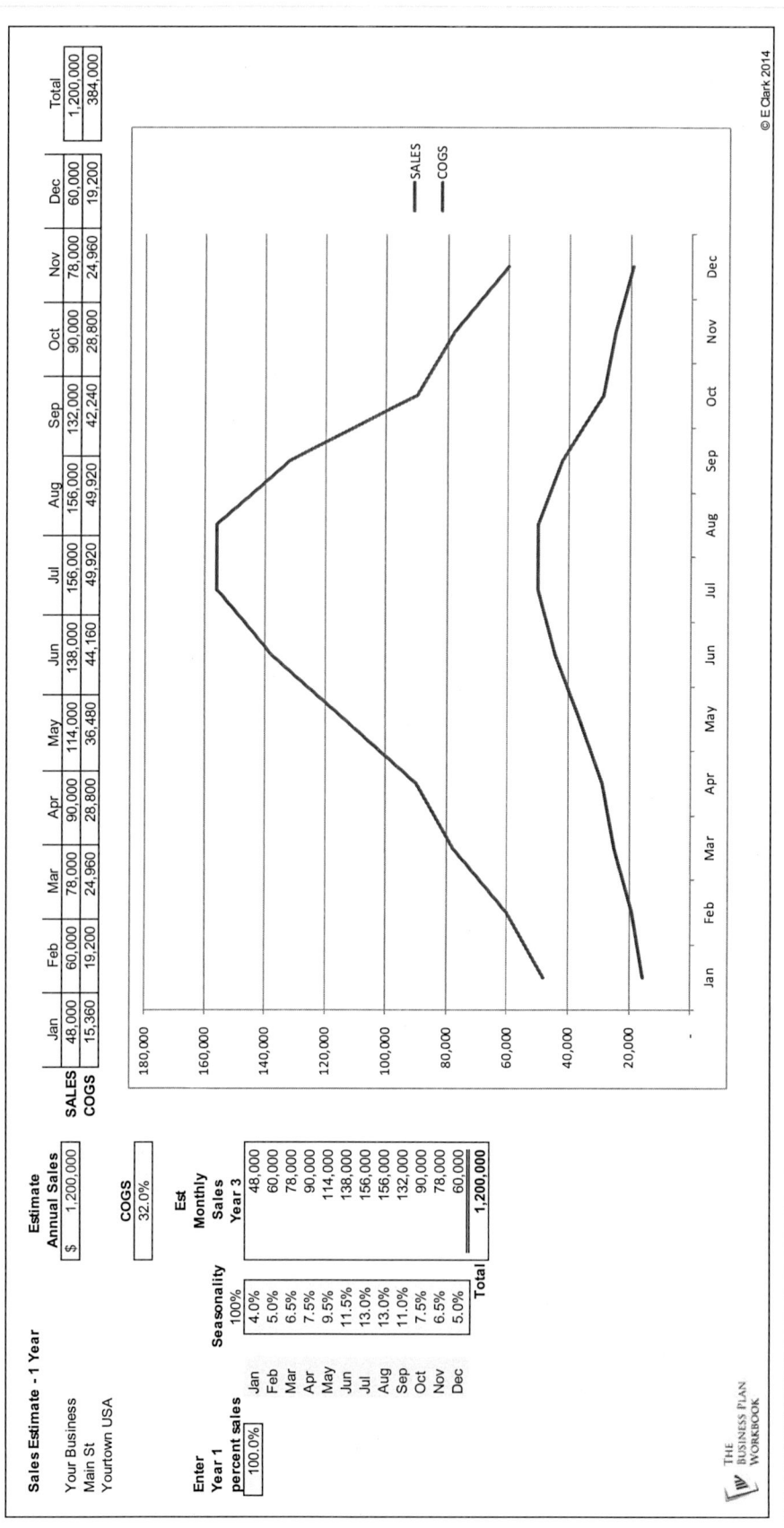

THE BUSINESS PLAN WORKBOOK

Financial Worksheet Templates

Sales Estimates – by product

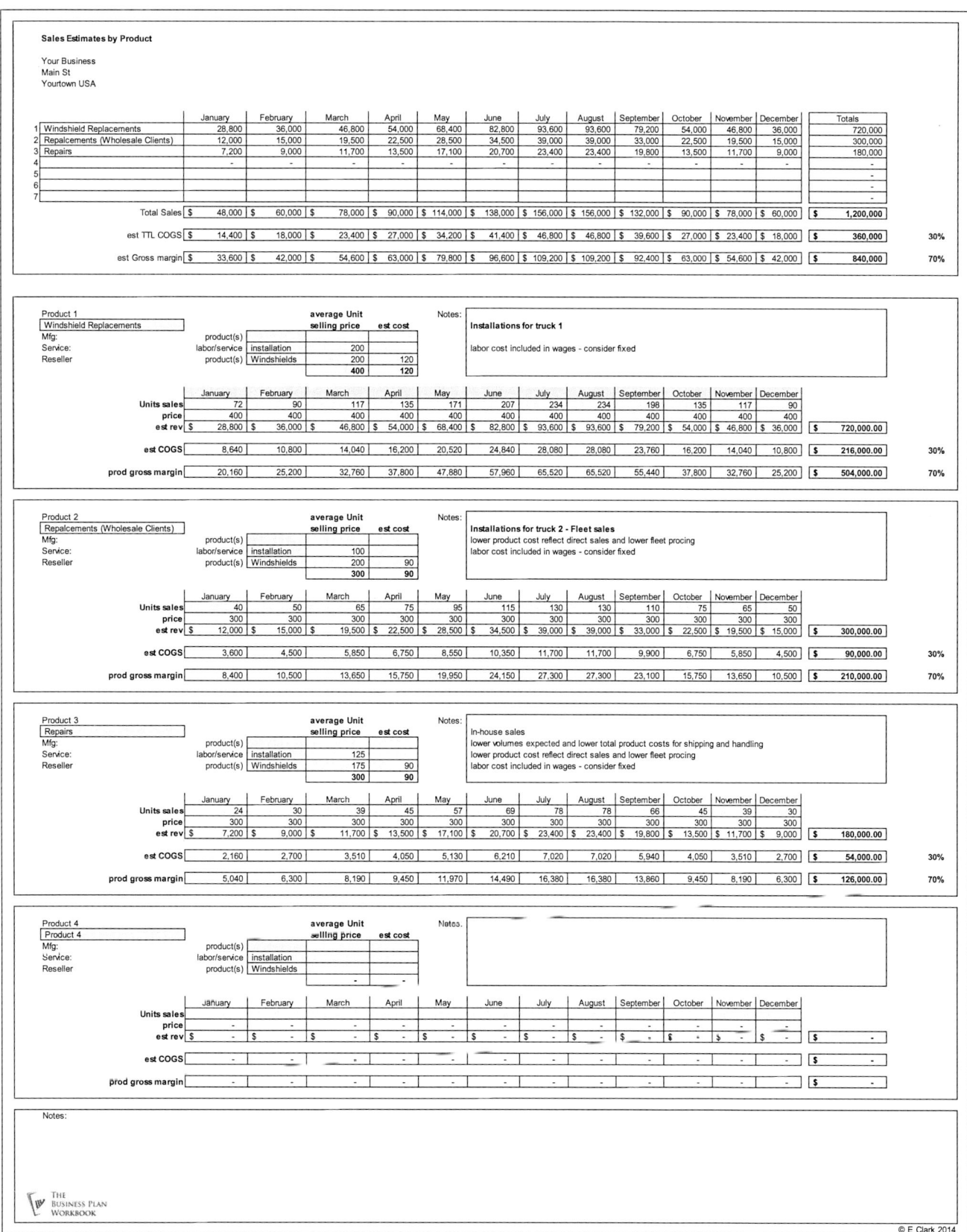

Sales Estimates by Product

Your Business
Main St
Yourtown USA

	January	February	March	April	May	June	July	August	September	October	November	December		Totals
1 Windshield Replacements	28,800	36,000	46,800	54,000	68,400	82,800	93,600	93,600	79,200	54,000	46,800	36,000		720,000
2 Repalcements (Wholesale Clients)	12,000	15,000	19,500	22,500	28,500	34,500	39,000	39,000	33,000	22,500	19,500	15,000		300,000
3 Repairs	7,200	9,000	11,700	13,500	17,100	20,700	23,400	23,400	19,800	13,500	11,700	9,000		180,000
4	-	-	-	-	-	-	-	-	-	-	-	-		-
5														-
6														-
7														-
Total Sales	$ 48,000	$ 60,000	$ 78,000	$ 90,000	$ 114,000	$ 138,000	$ 156,000	$ 156,000	$ 132,000	$ 90,000	$ 78,000	$ 60,000	$	1,200,000
est TTL COGS	$ 14,400	$ 18,000	$ 23,400	$ 27,000	$ 34,200	$ 41,400	$ 46,800	$ 46,800	$ 39,600	$ 27,000	$ 23,400	$ 18,000	$	360,000	30%
est Gross margin	$ 33,600	$ 42,000	$ 54,600	$ 63,000	$ 79,800	$ 96,600	$ 109,200	$ 109,200	$ 92,400	$ 63,000	$ 54,600	$ 42,000	$	840,000	70%

Product 1

Windshield Replacements

		average Unit selling price	est cost	Notes:
Mfg:	product(s)			Installations for truck 1
Service:	labor/service installation	200		labor cost included in wages - consider fixed
Reseller	product(s) Windshields	200	120	
		400	120	

	January	February	March	April	May	June	July	August	September	October	November	December		
Units sales	72	90	117	135	171	207	234	234	198	135	117	90		
price	400	400	400	400	400	400	400	400	400	400	400	400		
est rev	$ 28,800	$ 36,000	$ 46,800	$ 54,000	$ 68,400	$ 82,800	$ 93,600	$ 93,600	$ 79,200	$ 54,000	$ 46,800	$ 36,000	$	720,000.00
est COGS	8,640	10,800	14,040	16,200	20,520	24,840	28,080	28,080	23,760	16,200	14,040	10,800	$	216,000.00	30%
prod gross margin	20,160	25,200	32,760	37,800	47,880	57,960	65,520	65,520	55,440	37,800	32,760	25,200	$	504,000.00	70%

Product 2

Repalcements (Wholesale Clients)

		average Unit selling price	est cost	Notes:
Mfg:	product(s)			Installations for truck 2 - Fleet sales
Service:	labor/service installation	100		lower product cost reflect direct sales and lower fleet procing
Reseller	product(s) Windshields	200	90	labor cost included in wages - consider fixed
		300	90	

	January	February	March	April	May	June	July	August	September	October	November	December		
Units sales	40	50	65	75	95	115	130	130	110	75	65	50		
price	300	300	300	300	300	300	300	300	300	300	300	300		
est rev	$ 12,000	$ 15,000	$ 19,500	$ 22,500	$ 28,500	$ 34,500	$ 39,000	$ 39,000	$ 33,000	$ 22,500	$ 19,500	$ 15,000	$	300,000.00
est COGS	3,600	4,500	5,850	6,750	8,550	10,350	11,700	11,700	9,900	6,750	5,850	4,500	$	90,000.00	30%
prod gross margin	8,400	10,500	13,650	15,750	19,950	24,150	27,300	27,300	23,100	15,750	13,650	10,500	$	210,000.00	70%

Product 3

Repairs

		average Unit selling price	est cost	Notes:
Mfg:	product(s)			In-house sales
Service:	labor/service installation	125		lower volumes expected and lower total product costs for shipping and handling
Reseller	product(s) Windshields	175	90	lower product cost reflect direct sales and lower fleet procing
		300	90	labor cost included in wages - consider fixed

	January	February	March	April	May	June	July	August	September	October	November	December		
Units sales	24	30	39	45	57	69	78	78	66	45	39	30		
price	300	300	300	300	300	300	300	300	300	300	300	300		
est rev	$ 7,200	$ 9,000	$ 11,700	$ 13,500	$ 17,100	$ 20,700	$ 23,400	$ 23,400	$ 19,800	$ 13,500	$ 11,700	$ 9,000	$	180,000.00
est COGS	2,160	2,700	3,510	4,050	5,130	6,210	7,020	7,020	5,940	4,050	3,510	2,700	$	54,000.00	30%
prod gross margin	5,040	6,300	8,190	9,450	11,970	14,490	16,380	16,380	13,860	9,450	8,190	6,300	$	126,000.00	70%

Product 4

Product 4

		average Unit selling price	est cost	Notes:
Mfg:	product(s)			
Service:	labor/service installation			
Reseller	product(s) Windshields			
		-	-	

	January	February	March	April	May	June	July	August	September	October	November	December		
Units sales	-	-	-	-	-	-	-	-	-	-	-	-		
price	-	-	-	-	-	-	-	-	-	-	-	-		
est rev	$ -	$ -	$ -	$ -	$ -	$ -	$ -	$ -	$ -	$ -	$ -	$ -	$	-
est COGS	-	-	-	-	-	-	-	-	-	-	-	-	$	-
prod gross margin	-	-	-	-	-	-	-	-	-	-	-	-	$	-

Notes:

Income Statement

Income Statement

Your Business
Main St
Yourtown USA

Year 1   7/11/14

MONTH	Jan	Feb	Mar	Apr	May	Jun	Jul	Aug	Sep	Oct	Nov	Dec	TOTAL	%
Total Sales	24,000	30,000	39,000	45,000	57,000	69,000	78,000	78,000	66,000	45,000	39,000	30,000	600,000	100%
Cost of Goods Sold	7,680	9,600	12,480	14,400	18,240	22,080	24,960	24,960	21,120	14,400	12,480	9,600	192,000	32%
Gross Profit	16,320	20,400	26,520	30,600	38,760	46,920	53,040	53,040	44,880	30,600	26,520	20,400	408,000	68.0%
Operating Expenses														
1 Wages - Salaries	10,440	10,440	10,440	13,920	13,920	13,920	13,920	13,920	13,920	13,920	13,920	13,920	156,600	26.1%
2 Rent	2,800	2,800	2,800	2,800	2,800	2,800	2,800	2,800	2,800	2,800	2,800	2,800	33,600	5.6%
3 Utilities, elec	2,800	2,800	2,800	2,800	2,800	2,800	2,800	2,800	2,800	2,800	2,800	2,800	33,600	5.6%
4 Sales, General and Admin	1,800	1,800	1,800	1,800	1,800	1,800	1,800	1,800	1,800	1,800	1,800	1,800	21,600	3.6%
5 Accounting / Legal	600	600	600	600	600	600	600	600	600	600	600	600	7,200	1.2%
6 Mktg - Promotion	1,400	900	800	1,500	800	600	700	900	800	1,500	400	600	11,500	1.9%
7 Insurance	900	900	900	900	900	900	900	900	900	900	900	900	10,800	1.8%
8 Auto Expenses	900	900	900	900	900	900	900	900	900	900	900	900	10,800	1.8%
9 L-T Loan	-	2,090	2,090	2,090	2,090	2,090	2,090	2,090	2,090	2,090	2,090	2,090	22,991	3.8%
10 S-T Loan	-	2,756	3,586	3,940	3,940	3,940	3,940	3,940	3,940	3,940	3,940	3,940	41,799	7.0%
11 Operating Supplies	340	340	340	340	340	340	340	340	340	340	340	340	4,080	0.7%
12 Repairs/ Maintenance	200	200	200	200	200	200	200	200	200	200	200	200	2,400	0.4%
13 Depreciation	4,800	4,800	4,800	4,800	4,800	4,800	4,800	4,800	4,800	4,800	4,800	4,800	57,600	9.6%
14													-	
15													-	
16													-	
17													-	
18													-	
19													-	
20													-	
Total Expenses	26,980	31,326	32,056	36,590	35,890	35,990	35,790	35,990	35,890	36,590	35,490	35,990	414,570	69.1%
Net Profit Before Tax	(10,660)	(10,926)	(5,536)	(5,990)	2,870	10,930	17,250	17,050	8,990	(5,990)	(8,970)	(15,590)	(6,570)	-1.1%

Notes:

THE BUSINESS PLAN WORKBOOK

© E.Clark 2014

Financial Worksheet Templates

Cash flow Statement

Cash Flow Year 1 — 7/1/14

Your Business
Main St
Yourtown USA

MONTH	Start Up	Jan	Feb	Mar	Apr	May	Jun	Jul	Aug	Sep	Oct	Nov	Dec	TOTAL	%
Income from Sales															
Cash Receipts/Sales		24,000	30,000	39,000	45,000	57,000	69,000	78,000	78,000	66,000	45,000	39,000	30,000	600,000	100%
Disbursements															
1 Inventory (COGS)		7,680	9,600	12,480	14,400	18,240	22,080	24,960	24,960	21,120	14,400	12,480	9,600	192,000	32%
2 Wages - Salaries		10,440	10,440	10,440	13,920	13,920	13,920	13,920	13,920	13,920	13,920	13,920	13,920	156,600	26%
3 Rent		2,800	2,800	2,800	2,800	2,800	2,800	2,800	2,800	2,800	2,800	2,800	2,800	33,600	6%
4 Utilities, elec		3,400	3,400	3,400	3,400	3,400	3,400	3,400	3,400	3,400	3,400	3,400	3,400	40,800	7%
5 Sales, General and Admin		2,600	2,600	2,600	2,600	2,600	2,600	2,600	2,600	2,600	2,600	2,600	2,600	31,200	5%
6 Accounting / Legal		800	900	800	800	800	800	800	800	800	800	800	800	9,600	2%
7 Mktg - Promotion		1,400	900	800	1,500	800	900	800	900	800	1,500	400	800	11,500	2%
8 Insurance		1,500	1,500	1,500	1,500	1,500	1,500	1,500	1,500	1,500	1,500	1,500	1,500	18,000	3%
9 Auto Expenses		1,800	1,800	1,800	1,800	1,800	1,800	1,800	1,800	1,800	1,800	1,800	1,800	21,600	4%
10 L-T Loan		2,090	2,090	2,090	2,090	2,090	2,090	2,090	2,090	2,090	2,090	2,090	2,090	25,081	4%
11 S-T Loan		-	2,756	3,586	3,940	3,940	3,940	3,940	3,940	3,940	3,940	3,940	3,940	41,799	7%
12 Operating Supplies		340	340	340	340	340	340	340	340	340	340	340	340	4,080	1%
13 Repairs/ Maintenance		350	350	350	350	350	350	350	350	350	350	350	350	4,200	1%
Depreciation														-	
14															
15															
16															
17															
18															
19															
20														-	0%
Total Disbursed		35,200	39,376	42,986	49,440	52,580	56,520	59,200	59,400	55,460	49,440	46,420	44,040	590,060	98%
Cash flow from Operations		(11,200)	(9,376)	(3,986)	(4,440)	4,420	12,480	18,800	18,600	10,540	(4,440)	(7,420)	(14,040)		

Cash flow from Financing

	Start Up	Jan	Feb	Mar	Apr		Year 1	
L-T Loan Receipts	200,000						24,600	Line of Credit
S-T Loan Receipts	20,000	11,200	9,400	4,000	4,500		4,500	
Equity Invested	83,550							
Cash flow from Financing	303,550	11,200	9,400	4,000	4,500			

Start up Expenses:

	Start Up		Year 1
Capital Equipment List	250,000		-
One Time Start up Costs	14,900		-
Misc Equipment	3,100		-
Supplies and Expenses	15,550	#	-
Inventory	20,000	#	-
Total Start up Expenses	303,550		-

	Start Up	Jan	Feb	Mar	Apr	May	Jun	Jul	Aug	Sep	Oct	Nov	Dec
NET Cash flow	-	(0)	24	14	60	4,420	12,480	18,800	18,600	10,540	(4,440)	(7,420)	(14,040)
Beginning Cash Balance		-	(0)	24	37	98	4,518	16,998	35,798	54,399	64,939	60,499	53,079
Ending Cash Balance	-	(0)	24	37	98	4,518	16,998	35,798	54,399	64,939	60,499	53,079	39,040

Notes:

THE BUSINESS PLAN WORKBOOK

The Business Plan Workbook

Balance Sheet

| Balance Sheet | Year 1 | | | | 7/1/14 |

Your Business
Main St
Yourtown USA

	END OF Day 0	END OF Day 1	END OF year 1	END OF year 2	END OF year 3
ASSETS					
CURRENT ASSETS					
Cash	303,550.00				
Inventory					
Accounts Receievable					
Supplies					
Rent Deposit					
Tel Deposit					
Util Deposit					
Misc equipment					
TOTAL CURRENT ASSETS	303,550.00				
FIXED ASSETS					
Long Term Investments					
Property & Plant					
Goodwill					
Machinery & Equipment					
Less Depreciation (accumulated)					
TOTAL FIXED ASSETS	-				
TOTAL ASSETS	303,550.00				
LIABILITIES					
CURRENT LIABILITIES					
Bank loans (short-term)	20,000.00				
Wages Payable					
TOTAL CURRENT LIABILITIES	20,000.00				
LONG-TERM LIABILITIES					
Bank Loans Payable	200,000.00				
Notes Payable					
TOTAL LONG-TERM LIABILITIES	200,000.00				
TOTAL LIABILITIES	220,000.00				
OWNERS' EQUITY					
Owners Capital	83,550.00				-
Retained earnings					
TOTAL OWNERS' EQUITY	83,550.00			-	-
TOTAL LIABILITIES & OWNERS' EQUITY	303,550.00	-	-	-	-

Notes:

Assumptions:

THE
BUSINESS PLAN
WORKBOOK

© E Clark 2014

Financial Worksheet Templates

Statement of Shareholders' Equity

Statement of Shareholders' Equity		7/1/14
for the period ending	END OF PERIOD	
Your Business		
Main St		
Yourtown USA		

	Beginning Equity	START of PERIOD	
plus:	Equity Investments		
plus:	net income for	YEAR	
less:	Dividends for	YEAR	
	Ending Equity	END OF PERIOD	$ -

Operating Expenses

Operating Expenses

Line 1 Wages - Salaries

	Jan	Feb	Mar	Apr	May	Jun	Jul	Aug	Sep	Oct	Nov	Dec	TOTAL	%
Year 1	10,440	10,440	10,440	13,920	13,920	13,920	13,920	13,920	13,920	13,920	13,920	13,920	156,600	26.10%
Year 2	13,920	13,920	13,920	24,312	24,312	24,312	24,312	24,312	17,400	17,400	17,400	17,400	232,920	27.73%
Year 3	17,400	17,400	17,400	27,792	27,792	27,792	27,792	27,792	20,880	20,880	20,880	20,880	274,680	22.89%

Line 2 Rent

	Jan	Feb	Mar	Apr	May	Jun	Jul	Aug	Sep	Oct	Nov	Dec	TOTAL	%
Year 1	2,800	2,800	2,800	2,800	2,800	2,800	2,800	2,800	2,800	2,800	2,800	2,800	33,600	5.60%
Year 2	2,800	2,800	2,800	2,800	2,800	2,800	2,800	2,800	2,800	2,800	2,800	2,800	33,600	4.00%
Year 3	2,800	2,800	2,800	2,800	2,800	2,800	2,800	2,800	2,800	2,800	2,800	2,800	33,600	2.80%

Line 3 Utilities, elec

	Jan	Feb	Mar	Apr	May	Jun	Jul	Aug	Sep	Oct	Nov	Dec	TOTAL	%
Year 1	2,800	2,800	2,800	2,800	2,800	2,800	2,800	2,800	2,800	2,800	2,800	2,800	33,600	5.60%
Year 2	3,200	3,200	3,200	3,200	3,200	3,200	3,200	3,200	3,200	3,200	3,200	3,200	38,400	4.57%
Year 3	3,400	3,400	3,400	3,400	3,400	3,400	3,400	3,400	3,400	3,400	3,400	3,400	40,800	3.40%

Line 4 Sales, General and Admin

	Jan	Feb	Mar	Apr	May	Jun	Jul	Aug	Sep	Oct	Nov	Dec	TOTAL	%
Year 1	1,800	1,800	1,800	1,800	1,800	1,800	1,800	1,800	1,800	1,800	1,800	1,800	21,600	3.60%
Year 2	2,200	2,200	2,200	2,200	2,200	2,200	2,200	2,200	2,200	2,200	2,200	2,200	26,400	3.14%
Year 3	2,600	2,600	2,600	2,600	2,600	2,600	2,600	2,600	2,600	2,600	2,600	2,600	31,200	2.60%

Line 5 Accounting / Legal

	Jan	Feb	Mar	Apr	May	Jun	Jul	Aug	Sep	Oct	Nov	Dec	TOTAL	%
Year 1	600	600	600	600	600	600	600	600	600	600	600	600	7,200	1.20%
Year 2	700	700	700	700	700	700	700	700	700	700	700	700	8,400	1.00%
Year 3	800	800	800	800	800	800	800	800	800	800	800	800	9,600	0.80%

Line 6 Mktg - Promotion

	Jan	Feb	Mar	Apr	May	Jun	Jul	Aug	Sep	Oct	Nov	Dec	TOTAL	%
Year 1	1,400	900	800	1,500	800	900	700	900	800	1,500	400	900	11,500	1.92%
Year 2	1,400	900	800	1,500	800	900	700	900	800	1,500	400	900	11,500	1.37%
Year 3	1,400	900	800	1,500	800	900	700	900	800	1,500	400	900	11,500	0.96%

Line 7 Insurance

	Jan	Feb	Mar	Apr	May	Jun	Jul	Aug	Sep	Oct	Nov	Dec	TOTAL	%
Year 1	900	900	900	900	900	900	900	900	900	900	900	900	10,800	1.80%
Year 2	1,200	1,200	1,200	1,200	1,200	1,200	1,200	1,200	1,200	1,200	1,200	1,200	14,400	1.71%
Year 3	1,500	1,500	1,500	1,500	1,500	1,500	1,500	1,500	1,500	1,500	1,500	1,500	18,000	1.50%

Line 8 Auto Expenses

	Jan	Feb	Mar	Apr	May	Jun	Jul	Aug	Sep	Oct	Nov	Dec	TOTAL	%
Year 1	900	900	900	900	900	900	900	900	900	900	900	900	10,800	1.80%
Year 2	1,400	1,400	1,400	1,400	1,400	1,400	1,400	1,400	1,400	1,400	1,400	1,400	16,800	2.00%
Year 3	1,800	1,800	1,800	1,800	1,800	1,800	1,800	1,800	1,800	1,800	1,800	1,800	21,600	1.80%

Line 9 Operating Supplies

	Jan	Feb	Mar	Apr	May	Jun	Jul	Aug	Sep	Oct	Nov	Dec	TOTAL	%
Year 1	800	800	800	800	800	800	800	800	800	800	800	800	9,600	1.60%
Year 2	800	800	800	800	800	800	800	800	800	800	800	800	9,600	1.14%
Year 3	800	800	800	800	800	800	800	800	800	800	800	800	9,600	0.80%

Wages/Salaries

Employee Wages and Salaries   7/1/14

Your Business
Main St
Yourtown USA

Year 1

Staff		Jan	Feb	Mar	Apr	May	Jun	Jul	Aug	Sep	Oct	Nov	Dec
	employees	1	1	1	2	2	2	2	2	2	2	2	2
	mo. wage	2,400.00	2,400.00	2,400.00	2,400.00	2,400.00	2,400.00	2,400.00	2,400.00	2,400.00	2,400.00	2,400.00	2,400.00
taxes/benefits	ttl wages	2,400.00	2,400.00	2,400.00	4,800.00	4,800.00	4,800.00	4,800.00	4,800.00	4,800.00	4,800.00	4,800.00	4,800.00
0.45	taxes/benefits	1,080.00	1,080.00	1,080.00	2,160.00	2,160.00	2,160.00	2,160.00	2,160.00	2,160.00	2,160.00	2,160.00	2,160.00
	Total Benfits & Wages	3,480.00	3,480.00	3,480.00	6,960.00	6,960.00	6,960.00	6,960.00	6,960.00	6,960.00	6,960.00	6,960.00	6,960.00
Line	employees	2	2	2	2	2	2	2	2	2	2	2	2
	mo. wage	2,400.00	2,400.00	2,400.00	2,400.00	2,400.00	2,400.00	2,400.00	2,400.00	2,400.00	2,400.00	2,400.00	2,400.00
taxes/benefits	ttl wages	4,800.00	4,800.00	4,800.00	4,800.00	4,800.00	4,800.00	4,800.00	4,800.00	4,800.00	4,800.00	4,800.00	4,800.00
0.45	taxes/benefits	2,160.00	2,160.00	2,160.00	2,160.00	2,160.00	2,160.00	2,160.00	2,160.00	2,160.00	2,160.00	2,160.00	2,160.00
	Total Benfits & Wages	6,960.00	6,960.00	6,960.00	6,960.00	6,960.00	6,960.00	6,960.00	6,960.00	6,960.00	6,960.00	6,960.00	6,960.00
Part-time	employees	-	2		2	2	2	2	2	-	-	-	-
	hourly pay	12		-	-	-	-	-	-	-	-	-	-
	hours per month	-			120	120	120	120	120				
taxes/benefits	ttl wages	-	-	-	-	-	-	-	-	-	-	-	-
0.20	taxes/benefits	-	-	-	-	-	-	-	-	-	-	-	-
	Total Benfits & Wages	-	-	-	-	-	-	-	-	-	-	-	-
	Total Wages/Salaries	10,440.00	10,440.00	10,440.00	13,920.00	13,920.00	13,920.00	13,920.00	13,920.00	13,920.00	13,920.00	13,920.00	13,920.00

Total: 156,600.00

Year 2

Staff		Jan	Feb	Mar	Apr	May	Jun	Jul	Aug	Sep	Oct	Nov	Dec
	employees	2	2	2	2	2	2	2	2	2	2	2	2
	mo. wage	2,400.00	2,400.00	2,400.00	2,400.00	2,400.00	2,400.00	2,400.00	2,400.00	2,400.00	2,400.00	2,400.00	2,400.00
taxes/benefits	ttl wages	4,800.00	4,800.00	4,800.00	4,800.00	4,800.00	4,800.00	4,800.00	4,800.00	4,800.00	4,800.00	4,800.00	4,800.00
0.45	taxes/benefits	2,160.00	2,160.00	2,160.00	2,160.00	2,160.00	2,160.00	2,160.00	2,160.00	2,160.00	2,160.00	2,160.00	2,160.00
	Total Benfits & Wages	6,960.00	6,960.00	6,960.00	6,960.00	6,960.00	6,960.00	6,960.00	6,960.00	6,960.00	6,960.00	6,960.00	6,960.00
Line	employees	2	2	2	3	3	3	3	3	3	3	3	3
	mo. wage	2,400.00	2,400.00	2,400.00	2,400.00	2,400.00	2,400.00	2,400.00	2,400.00	2,400.00	2,400.00	2,400.00	2,400.00
taxes/benefits	ttl wages	4,800.00	4,800.00	4,800.00	7,200.00	7,200.00	7,200.00	7,200.00	7,200.00	7,200.00	7,200.00	7,200.00	7,200.00
0.45	taxes/benefits	2,160.00	2,160.00	2,160.00	3,240.00	3,240.00	3,240.00	3,240.00	3,240.00	3,240.00	3,240.00	3,240.00	3,240.00
	Total Benfits & Wages	6,960.00	6,960.00	6,960.00	10,440.00	10,440.00	10,440.00	10,440.00	10,440.00	10,440.00	10,440.00	10,440.00	10,440.00
Part-time	employees	-			4	4	4	4	4	-			
	hourly pay	12	12	12	12	12	12	12	12	12	12	12	12
	hours per month	-			120	120	120	120	120				
taxes/benefits	ttl wages	-	-	-	5,760.00	5,760.00	5,760.00	5,760.00	5,760.00	-	-	-	-
0.20	taxes/benefits	-	-	-	1,152.00	1,152.00	1,152.00	1,152.00	1,152.00	-	-	-	-
	Total Benfits & Wages	-	-	-	6,912.00	6,912.00	6,912.00	6,912.00	6,912.00	-	-	-	-
	Total Wages/Salaries	13,920.00	13,920.00	13,920.00	24,312.00	24,312.00	24,312.00	24,312.00	24,312.00	17,400.00	17,400.00	17,400.00	17,400.00

Total: 232,920.00

Year 3

Staff		Jan	Feb	Mar	Apr	May	Jun	Jul	Aug	Sep	Oct	Nov	Dec
	employees	2	2	2	2	2	2	2	2	2	2	2	2
	mo. wage	2,400.00	2,400.00	2,400.00	2,400.00	2,400.00	2,400.00	2,400.00	2,400.00	2,400.00	2,400.00	2,400.00	2,400.00
taxes/benefits	ttl wages	4,800.00	4,800.00	4,800.00	4,800.00	4,800.00	4,800.00	4,800.00	4,800.00	4,800.00	4,800.00	4,800.00	4,800.00
0.45	taxes/benefits	2,160.00	2,160.00	2,160.00	2,160.00	2,160.00	2,160.00	2,160.00	2,160.00	2,160.00	2,160.00	2,160.00	2,160.00
	Total Benfits & Wages	6,960.00	6,960.00	6,960.00	6,960.00	6,960.00	6,960.00	6,960.00	6,960.00	6,960.00	6,960.00	6,960.00	6,960.00
Line	employees	3	3	3	4	4	4	4	4	4	4	4	4
	mo. wage	2,400.00	2,400.00	2,400.00	2,400.00	2,400.00	2,400.00	2,400.00	2,400.00	2,400.00	2,400.00	2,400.00	2,400.00
taxes/benefits	ttl wages	7,200.00	7,200.00	7,200.00	9,600.00	9,600.00	9,600.00	9,600.00	9,600.00	9,600.00	9,600.00	9,600.00	9,600.00
0.45	taxes/benefits	3,240.00	3,240.00	3,240.00	4,320.00	4,320.00	4,320.00	4,320.00	4,320.00	4,320.00	4,320.00	4,320.00	4,320.00
	Total Benfits & Wages	10,440.00	10,440.00	10,440.00	13,920.00	13,920.00	13,920.00	13,920.00	13,920.00	13,920.00	13,920.00	13,920.00	13,920.00
Part-time	employees	-			4	4	4	4	4				
	hourly pay	12	12	12	12	12	12	12	12	12	12	12	12
	hours per month	-			120	120	120	120	120				
taxes/benefits	ttl wages	-	-	-	5,700.00	5,760.00	5,760.00	5,760.00	5,760.00	-	-	-	-
0.20	taxes/benefits	-	-	-	1,152.00	1,152.00	1,152.00	1,152.00	1,152.00	-	-	-	-
	Total Benfits & Wages	-	-	-	6,912.00	6,912.00	6,912.00	6,912.00	6,912.00	-	-	-	-
	Total Wages/Salaries	17,400.00	17,400.00	17,400.00	27,792.00	27,792.00	27,792.00	27,792.00	27,792.00	20,880.00	20,880.00	20,880.00	20,880.00

Total: 274,680.00

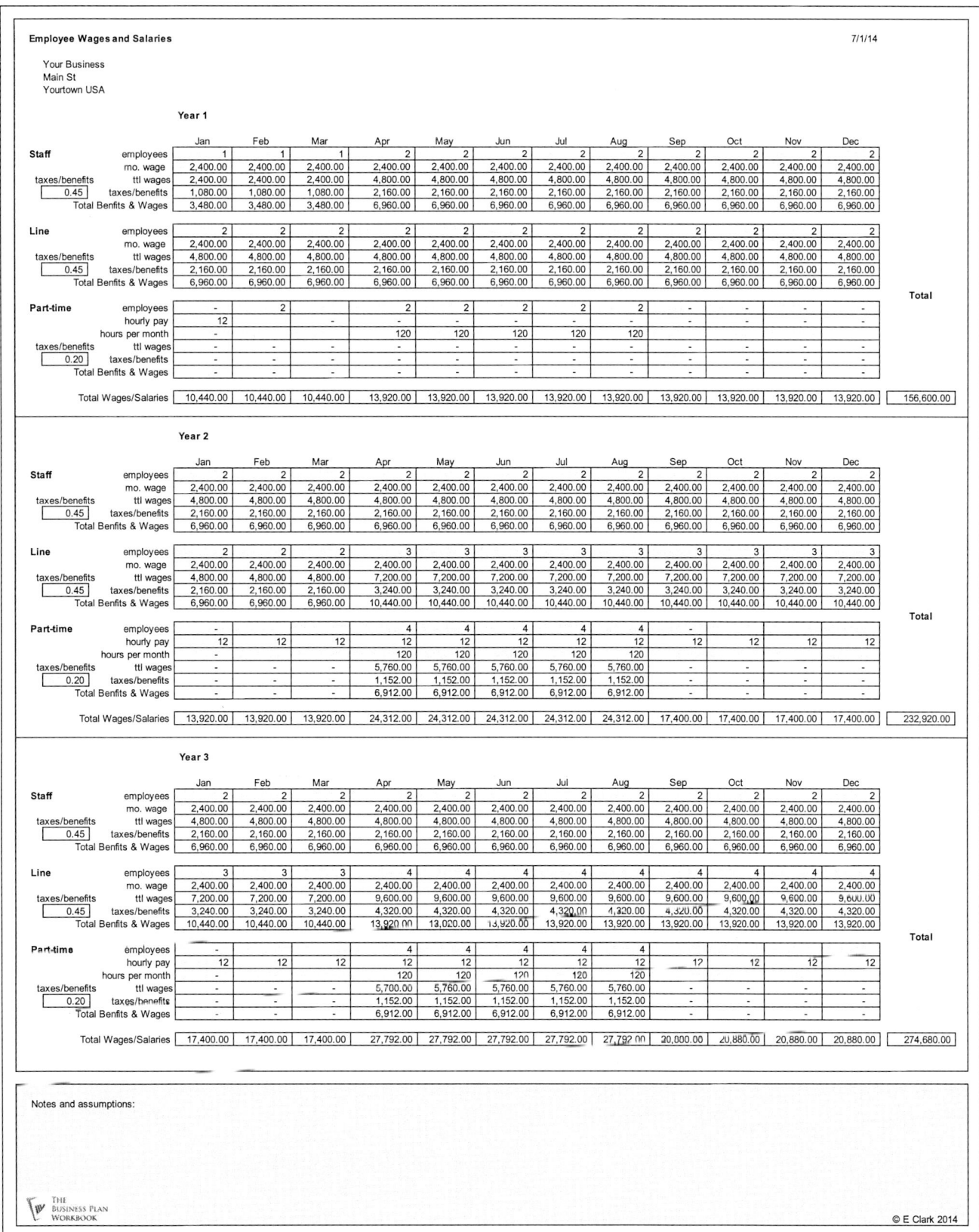

Notes and assumptions:

THE
BUSINESS PLAN
WORKBOOK

Inventory

Inventory Year 1 7/1/14

Your Business
Main St
Yourtown USA

MONTH	Jan	Feb	Mar	Apr	May	Jun	Jul	Aug	Sep	Oct	Nov	Dec	TOTAL	%
Beginning Inventory	20,000	23,800	23,800	23,800	23,800	23,800	23,800	23,800	23,800	23,800	23,800	23,800	281,800	100%
1 Product 1	10,000	10,000	10,000	10,000	10,000	10,000	10,000	10,000	10,000	10,000	10,000	10,000	120,000	38.8%
2 Product 2	5,000	5,000	5,000	5,000	5,000	5,000	5,000	5,000	5,000	5,000	5,000	5,000	60,000	19.4%
3 Product 3	4,000	4,000	4,000	4,000	4,000	4,000	4,000	4,000	4,000	4,000	4,000	4,000	48,000	15.5%
4 Product 4	3,000	3,000	3,000	3,000	3,000	3,000	3,000	3,000	3,000	3,000	3,000	3,000	36,000	11.6%
5 Product 5	2,000	2,000	2,000	2,000	2,000	2,000	2,000	2,000	2,000	2,000	2,000	2,000	24,000	7.8%
6 Product 6	1,000	1,000	1,000	1,000	1,000	1,000	1,000	1,000	1,000	1,000	1,000	1,000	12,000	3.9%
7 Product 7	500	500	500	500	500	500	500	500	500	500	500	500	6,000	1.9%
8 Product 8	300	300	300	300	300	300	300	300	300	300	300	300	3,600	1.2%
Inventory Purchased	25,800	25,800	25,800	25,800	25,800	25,800	25,800	25,800	25,800	25,800	25,800	25,800	309,600	
Cost of Goods Sold	22,000	25,800	25,800	25,800	25,800	25,800	25,800	25,800	25,800	25,800	25,800	25,800	305,800	
Ending Inventory	23,800	23,800	23,800	23,800	23,800	23,800	23,800	23,800	23,800	23,800	23,800	23,800	285,600	

Notes:

THE
BUSINESS PLAN
WORKBOOK

Financial Worksheet Templates

Marketing - Promotional Expenses

Promotion/Marketing Mix   7/1/14

Your Business
Main St
Yourtown USA

Promotion	Jan	Feb	Mar	Apr	May	Jun	Jul	Aug	Sep	Oct	Nov	Dec	Total
sponsorship	400.00		400.00		400.00				400.00				
product placement													
endorsements													
merchandising	100.00	100.00	100.00	100.00	100.00	100.00	100.00	100.00	100.00	100.00	100.00	100.00	
public relations													
trade shows													
Advertising													
TV	600.00												
radio				600.00			600.00			600.00			
newspapers		500.00		500.00		500.00		500.00		500.00		500.00	
Internet	300.00	300.00	300.00	300.00	300.00	300.00		300.00	300.00	300.00	300.00	300.00	
Mobile Phones													
	1,400.00	900.00	800.00	1,500.00	800.00	900.00	700.00	900.00	800.00	1,500.00	400.00	900.00	**Total** 11,500.00

Notes and assumptions:

THE BUSINESS PLAN WORKBOOK

© E Clark 2014

The Business Plan Workbook

Loan Repayment Schedule (long-term)

Long-Term Loan Repayment Schedule

7/1/14

Year 1

	Jan	Feb	Mar	Apr	May	Jun	Jul	Aug	Sep	Oct	Nov	Dec
Amount Borrowed	200,000				-	-	-	-	-	-	-	-
Principal												
interest rate	0.08											
term-months	96.00											
Total												
Loan 1		2,090.08	$2,090.08	$2,090.08	$2,090.08	$2,090.08	$2,090.08	$2,090.08	$2,090.08	$2,090.08	$2,090.08	$2,090.08
Loan 2												
Loan 3												
Loan 4												
Loan 5												

	Jan	Feb	Mar	Apr	May	Jun	Jul	Aug	Sep	Oct	Nov	Dec	Total
Total Loan Payment	-	2,090	2,090	2,090	2,090	2,090	2,090	2,090	2,090	2,090	2,090	2,090	22,990.88

Short-Term Loan Repayment Schedule

Year 2

	Jan	Feb	Mar	Apr	May	Jun	Jul	Aug	Sep	Oct	Nov	Dec
Amount Borrowed												
Principal												
interest rate												
term-months												
Total												
Loan 1	2,090.08	2,090.08	2,090.08	2,090.08	2,090.08	2,090.08	2,090.08	2,090.08	2,090.08	2,090.08	2,090.08	2,090.08
Loan 2												
Loan 3												
Loan 4												
Loan 5												
Loan 6												
Loan 7												
Loan 8												
Loan 9												
Loan 10												

	Jan	Feb	Mar	Apr	May	Jun	Jul	Aug	Sep	Oct	Nov	Dec	Total
Total Loan Payment	2,090.08	2,090	2,090	2,090	2,090	2,090	2,090	2,090	2,090	2,090	2,090	2,090	25,080.96

Short-Term Loan Repayment Schedule

Year 3

	Jan	Feb	Mar	Apr	May	Jun	Jul	Aug	Sep	Oct	Nov	Dec
Amount Borrowed	200,000											
Principal	200,000.00											
rate	0.08											
Interest term (months)	96.00											
Loan 1	2,090.08	2,090.08	2,090.08	2,090.08	2,090.08	2,090.08	2,090.08	2,090.08	2,090.08	2,090.08	2,090.08	2,090.08
Loan 2												
Loan 3												
Loan 4												
Loan 5												
Loan 6												
Loan 7												
Loan 8												
Loan 9												
Loan 10												

	Jan	Feb	Mar	Apr	May	Jun	Jul	Aug	Sep	Oct	Nov	Dec	Total
Total Loan Payment	2,090.08	2,090	2,090	2,090	2,090	2,090	2,090	2,090	2,090	2,090	2,090	2,090	25,080.96

Notes and assumptions:

Financial Worksheet Templates

Loan Repayment Schedule (short-term)

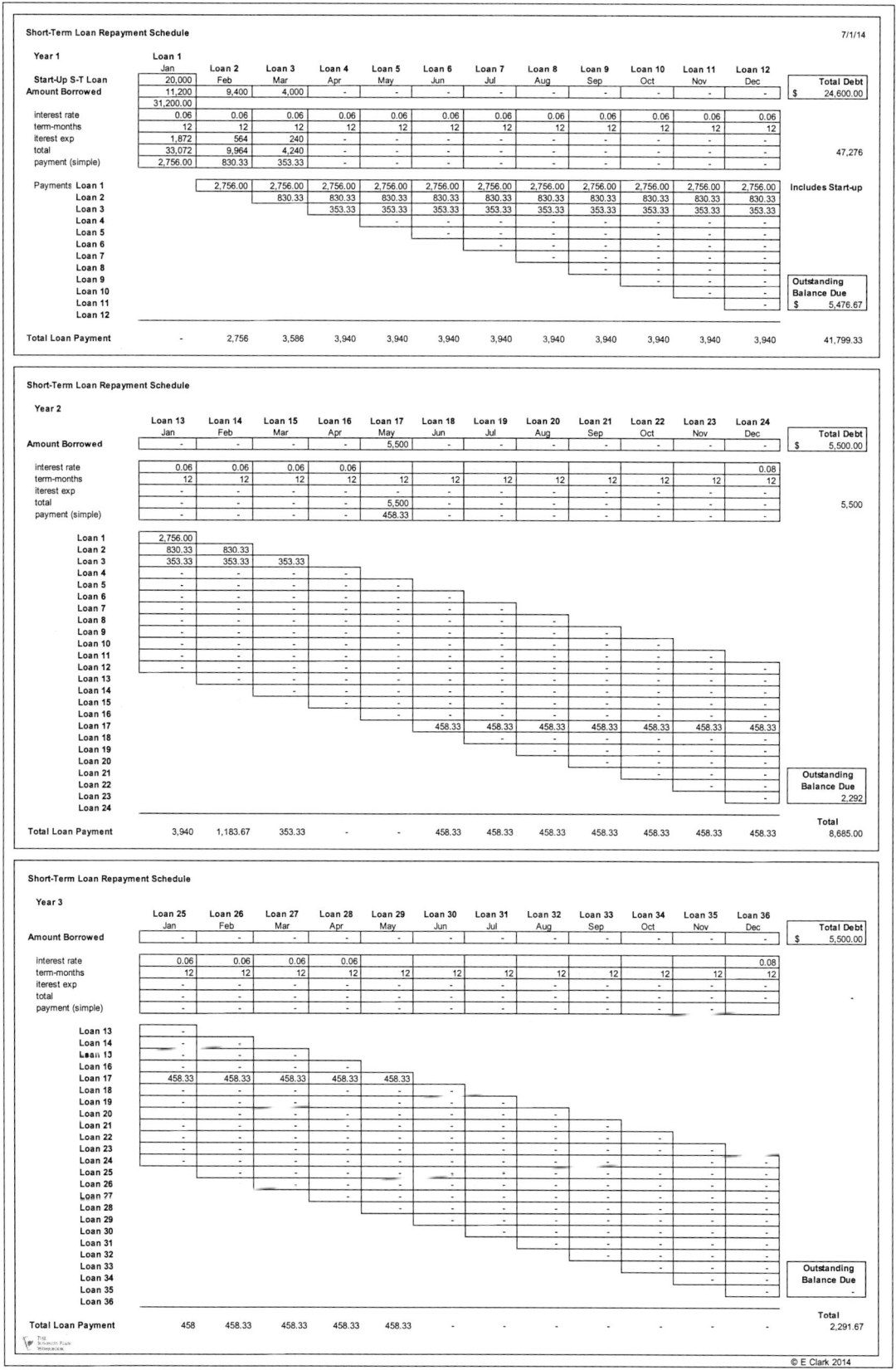

Depreciation Schedules

Depreciation Schedules

Your Business
Main St
Yourtown USA

7/1/14

Year 1

Asset	Book Value	depr. term mos.	Jan	Feb	Mar	Apr	May	Jun	Jul	Aug	Sep	Oct	Nov	Dec
asset 1 (identify)	480,000	100	4,800	4,800.00	4,800.00	4,800.00	4,800.00	4,800.00	4,800.00	4,800.00	4,800.00	4,800.00	4,800.00	4,800.00
asset 2 (identify)	-	-												
asset 3 (identify)	-	-												
asset 4 (identify)	-	-												
asset 5 (identify)	-	-												
asset 6 (identify)	-	-												
Total Monthly Depreciation			4,800.00	4,800.00	4,800.00	4,800.00	4,800.00	4,800.00	4,800.00	4,800.00	4,800.00	4,800.00	4,800.00	4,800.00

57,600.00

Year 2

Asset	Book Value	depr. term mos.	Jan	Feb	Mar	Apr	May	Jun	Jul	Aug	Sep	Oct	Nov	Dec
asset 1 (identify)			4,800	4,800	4,800	4,800	4,800	4,800	4,800	4,800	4,800	4,800	4,800	4,800
asset 2 (identify)			-	-	-	-	-	-	-	-	-	-	-	
asset 3 (identify)			-	-	-	-	-	-	-	-	-	-	-	
asset 4 (identify)			-	-	-	-	-	-	-	-	-	-	-	
asset 5 (identify)			-	-	-	-	-	-	-	-	-	-	-	
asset 6 (identify)			-	-	-	-	-	-	-	-	-	-	-	
Total Monthly Depreciation			4,800.00	4,800.00	4,800.00	4,800.00	4,800.00	4,800.00	4,800.00	4,800.00	4,800.00	4,800.00	4,800.00	4,800.00

57,600.00

Year 3

Asset	Book Value	depr. term mos.	Jan	Feb	Mar	Apr	May	Jun	Jul	Aug	Sep	Oct	Nov	Dec
asset 1 (identify)			4,800	4,800	4,800	4,800	4,800	4,800	4,800	4,800	4,800	4,800	4,800	4,800
asset 2 (identify)			-	-	-	-	-	-	-	-	-	-	-	
asset 3 (identify)			-	-	-	-	-	-	-	-	-	-	-	
asset 4 (identify)			-	-	-	-	-	-	-	-	-	-	-	
asset 5 (identify)			-	-	-	-	-	-	-	-	-	-	-	
asset 6 (identify)			-	-	-	-	-	-	-	-	-	-	-	
Total Monthly Depreciation			4,800.00	4,800.00	4,800.00	4,800.00	4,800.00	4,800.00	4,800.00	4,800.00	4,800.00	4,800.00	4,800.00	4,800.00

57,600.00

Notes and assumptions:

THE BUSINESS PLAN WORKBOOK

Financial Worksheet Templates

Operating Ratios

Financial Ratios   1/0/00

	Date	7/14/14
Your Business	as of	12/31/12
Main St	from	1/1/12
Yourtown USA	to	12/31/12

Liquidity Ratios

Current Ratio $= \dfrac{\text{current assets}}{\text{current liabilities}}$　$\dfrac{819,399}{578,444} = 1.42$

Quick Ratio $= \dfrac{(\text{ current assets - inventory })}{\text{current liabilities}}$　$\dfrac{(\quad 819,399\;-\;497,049\;)}{578,444} = 0.56$

Activity Ratios　　Asset Management Ratios

Inventory turnover $= \dfrac{\text{cost of goods sold}}{\text{average Inventory}}$　$\dfrac{192,000}{500,000} = 0.38$

Accounts Receivable Turnover $= \dfrac{\text{sales}}{\text{avg accts receivables}}$　$\dfrac{600,000}{56,234} = 10.67$

Avg Accts Receivables $=$ average of the current period balance and the previous period balance

Total asset utilization $= \dfrac{\text{sales}}{\text{total assets}}$　$\dfrac{600,000}{1,560,406} = 0.38$

Average Collection $= \dfrac{\text{accounts receivable}}{\text{average sales per day}}$　365　$\dfrac{56,234}{1,644} = 34.21$

Fixed Asset Turnover $= \dfrac{\text{sales}}{\text{net fixed assets}}$　$\dfrac{600,000}{741,008} = 0.81$

Total Asset Turnover $= \dfrac{\text{sales}}{\text{total assets}}$　$\dfrac{600,000}{1,560,406} = 0.38$

Profitability Ratios

Profit Margin on Sales $= \dfrac{\text{profit before tax}}{\text{sales}}$　$\dfrac{-}{600,000} = -$

Net Profit Margin $= \dfrac{\text{net income}}{\text{sales}}$　$\dfrac{(56,375)}{600,000} = (0.09)$

Asset Turnover $= \dfrac{\text{sales}}{\text{average assets}}$　$\dfrac{600,000}{-} =$ #DIV/0!

Return on Assets $= \dfrac{\text{net profit after taxes}}{\text{total assets}}$　$\dfrac{-}{1,560,406} = -$

Return on Total Assets $= \dfrac{\text{profit before tax}}{\text{total assets}}$　$\dfrac{-}{1,560,406} = -$

Leverage Ratios　　Solvency and Coverage Ratios

Debt to Equity $= \dfrac{\text{total debt}}{\text{total equity}}$　$\dfrac{1,371,917}{188,489} = 7.28$

Debt Ratio $= \dfrac{\text{total debt}}{\text{total Assets}}$　$\dfrac{1,371,917}{1,560,406} = 0.88$

Times Interest Earned $= \dfrac{\text{operating income}}{\text{interest expense}}$　$\dfrac{-}{64,420} = -$

Accounts Payable $= \dfrac{\text{ending A/P}}{\text{avg daily purchases}}$　$\dfrac{304,615}{-} =$ #DIV/0!

The Business Plan Workbo

Break Even Analysis

Break Even

7/14/14

Your Business
Main St
Yourtown USA

Est sales in Units	4000	
Selling price	$ 2.00	

Cost Description	Fixed Costs ($)	Variable Costs (%)
Variable Costs		
Cost of Goods Sold		$ 0.88
Raw Materials		$ 0.12
Direct Labor (Includes Payroll Taxes)		
Fixed Costs		
Salaries (includes payroll taxes)	$ 200.00	
Supplies		
Repairs & maintenance	$ 22.00	
Advertising		
Car, delivery and travel		
Accounting and legal		
Rent		
Telephone		
Utilities		
Insurance		
Taxes (Real estate, etc.)		
Interest		
Depreciation		
Other (specify)		
Other (specify)	$ -	
Miscellaneous expenses	$ -	
Principal portion of debt payment	$ -	
	$ -	
Total Fixed Costs	$ 222.00	
Total Variable Costs		$ 1.00

Break Even

$$\frac{FC}{Price - VC}$$

or

BE = FC / Gross Margin

$$\frac{\text{FIXED COSTS} \quad \$ \quad 222.00}{\text{Price - VC} \quad \$ \quad 1.00} = \$ \ 222.00 \ \text{BE PER YEAR}$$

$$\frac{\text{FIXED COSTS} \quad \$ \quad 222.00}{\text{GROSS MARGIN} \quad 60\%} = \$ \ 370.00 \ \text{BE PER YEAR}$$

Feasibility **Sales per day in Dollars**
$ 370.00 $ 1.48 PER DAY
250

Sales per day
$ 1.48 $ per day average sale   #DIV/0! sales/day

Notes:

© E Clark 2010

Notes and assumptions:

© E Clark 2014

Financial Worksheet Templates

THE
BUSINESS PLAN
WORKBOOK

THE
BUSINESS PLAN
WORKBOOK

For a complete set of linked excel Financial Templates visit:

www.TheBusinessPlanWorkbook.com

The Business Plan Workbook
for an Owner-Managed Business

A practical guide to creating an effective business plan for an owner-managed business